Bill Nye's Sparks

By

Edgar Wilson Nye (Bill Nye)

Bill Nye's Sparks
by Edgar Wilson Nye (Bill Nye)

ISBN: 978-93-61152-88-7

Published by

DOUBLE 9 BOOKS

2/13-B, Ansari Road
Daryaganj, New Delhi – 110002
info@double9books.com
www.double9books.com
Tel. 011-40042856

ABOUT THE AUTHOR

Edgar Wilson Nye was an American comedian, journalist, and columnist who published under the pen name Bill Nye. In the late 1800s, Bill Nye became well-known for his clever and amusing writings. He started his career as a journalist, contributing to a number of newspapers. It was a satirical column he founded called "The Boomerang" in the Laramie Boomerang, a daily published in Wyoming, that gave Nye his first break. As a result of this column's success, Nye gained national exposure and gained popularity as a humourist. Nye, who was well-known for his astute and humorous observations on ordinary life, wrote about a wide range of subjects, such as politics, society, and human nature. In addition, he gave funny lectures and lectured across the country, enhancing his standing as a well-liked comedian. As a trailblazer in American humour writing, Edgar Wilson Nye's writings are still valued for their ageless wit and humorous acumen.

CONTENTS

BIOGRAPHICAL

Edgar Wilson Nye was whole-souled, big-hearted and genial. Those who knew him lost sight of the humorist in the wholesome friend.

He was born August 25, 1850, in Shirley, Piscataquis County, Maine. Poverty of resources drove the family to St. Croix Valley, Wisconsin, where they hoped to be able to live under conditions less severe. After receiving a meager schooling, he entered a lawyer's office where most of his work consisted in sweeping the office and running errands. In his idle moments the lawyer's library was at his service. Of this crude and desultory reading he afterward wrote:

"I could read the same passage today that I did yesterday and it would seem as fresh at the second reading as it did at the first. On the following day I could read it again and it would seem as new and mysterious as it did on the preceding day."

At the age of twenty-five, he was teaching a district school in Polk County, Wisconsin, at thirty dollars a month. In 1877 he was justice of the peace in Laramie. Of that experience he wrote:

"It was really pathetic to see the poor little miserable booth where I sat and waited with numb fingers for business. But I did not see the pathos which clung to every cobweb and darkened the rattling casement. Possibly I did not know enough. I forgot to say the office was not a salaried one, but solely dependent upon fees. So while I was called Judge Nye and frequently mentioned in the papers with consideration, I was out of coal half the time, and once could not mail my letters for three weeks because I did not have the necessary postage."

He wrote some letters to the Cheyenne *Sun* and soon made such a reputation for himself that he was able to obtain a position on the Laramie *Sentinel*. Of this experience he wrote:

"The salary was small, but the latitude was great, and I was permitted to write anything that I thought would please the people, whether it was news or not. By and by I had won every heart by my patient poverty and my delightful parsimony with regards to facts. With a hectic imagination and an order on a restaurant which advertised in the paper I scarcely cared through the livelong day whether school kept or not."

Of the proprietor of the *Sentinel* he wrote:

"I don't know whether he got into the penitentiary or the Greenback party. At any rate he was the wickedest man in Wyoming. Still, he was warm-hearted and generous to a fault. He was more generous to a fault than to anything else—more especially his own faults. He gave me twelve dollars a week to edit the paper—local, telegraph, selections, religious, sporting, political, fashions, and obituary. He said twelve dollars was too much, but if I would jerk the press occasionally and take care of his children he would try to stand it. You can't mix politics and measles. I saw that I would have to draw the line at measles. So one day I drew my princely salary and quit, having acquired a style of fearless and independent journalism which I still retain. I can write up things that never occurred with a masterly and graphic hand. Then, if they occur, I am grateful; if not, I bow to the inevitable and smother my chagrin."

In the midst of a wrangle in politics he was appointed postmaster of his town and his letter of acceptance, addressed to the Postmaster-General at Washington, was the first of his writings to attract national attention.

He said that, in his opinion, his being selected for the office was a triumph of eternal right over error and wrong. "It is one of the epochs, I may say, in the nation's onward march toward political purity and perfection," he wrote. "I don't know when I have noticed any stride in the affairs of state which has so thoroughly impressed me with its wisdom."

Shortly after he became postmaster he started the *Boomerang*. The first office of the paper was over a livery stable and Nye put up a sign instructing callers to "twist the tail of the gray mule and take the elevator."

He at once became famous and was soon brought to New York, at a salary that seemed fabulous to him. His place among the humorists of the world was thenceforth assured.

He died February 22, 1896, at his home in North Carolina, surrounded by his family.

James Whitcomb Riley, the Hoosier poet, was for many years a close personal friend of the dead humorist. When informed of Nye's death, he said: "Especially favored, as for years I have been, with close personal acquaintance and association with Mr. Nye, his going away fills me with selfishness of grief that finds a mute rebuke in my every memory of him. He was unselfish wholly, and I am broken-hearted, recalling the always patient strength and gentleness of this true man, the unfailing hope and cheer and faith of his child-heart, his noble and heroic life, and pure devotion to his home his deep affections, constant dreams, plans and realizations. I cannot doubt but that somehow, somewhere, he continues cheerily on in the unbroken exercise of these same capacities."

Mr. Riley recently wrote the following sonnet:

> O William, in thy blithe companionship
> What liberty is mine — what sweet release
> From clamourous strife, and yet, what boisterous peace!
> Ho! ho! It is thy fancy's finger tip
> That dints the dimple now, and kinks the lip
> That scarce may sing in all this glad increase
> Of merriment! So, pray thee, do not cease
> To cheer me thus, for underneath the quip
> Of thy droll sorcery the wrangling fret
> Of all distress is still. No syllable
> Of sorrow vexeth me, no tear drops wet
> My teeming lids, save those that leap to tell
> Thee thou'st a guest that overweepeth yet
> Only because thou jokest overwell.

REQUESTING A REMITTANCE

[Personal]

Washington, D. C.

Along toward morning, 1887.

Cashier World Office, New York.—

MY DEAR SIR: You will doubtless be surprised to hear from me so soon, as I did not promise when I left New York that I would write you at all while here. But now I take pen in hand to say that the Senate and House of Representatives are having a good deal of fun with me, and hope you are enjoying the same great blessing. You will wonder at first why I send in my expense account before I send in anything for the paper, but I will explain that to you when I get back. At first I thought I would not bother with the expense account till I got to your office, but I can now see that it is going to worry me to get there unless I hear from you favorably by return mail.

When I came here I fell into the mad whirl of society, and attracted a good deal of attention by my cultivated ways and Jeffersonian method of sleeping with a different member of Congress every night.

I have not written anything for publication yet, but I am getting material together that will make people throughout our broad land open their eyes in astonishment. I shall deal fairly and openly with these great national questions, and frankly hew to the line, let the chips fall where they may, as I heard a man say to-day on the floor of the house—the Willard House, I mean. But I believe in handling great political matters without gloves, as you will remember, if you have watched my course as justice of the peace and litterateur. Candor is my leading characteristic, and if you will pardon me for saying so in the first letter you ever received from me I believe there is nothing about my whole character which seems to challenge my admiration for myself any more than that.

Congressmen and their wives are daily landing at the great national Castle Garden and looking wildly around for the place where they are told they will get their mileage. On every hand all is hurry and excitement.

Bills are being introduced, acquaintances renewed, and punch bowls are beginning to wear a preoccupied air.

I have been mingling with society ever since I came here, and that is one reason I have written very little for publication, and did not send what I did write.

Yesterday afternoon my money gave out at 3:20, and since that my mind has been clearer and society has made fewer demands on me. At first I thought I would obtain employment at the Treasury Department as exchange editor in the greenback room. Then I remembered that I would get very faint before I could go through a competitive examination, and, in the meantime, I might lose social caste by wearing my person on the outside of my clothes. So I have resolved to write you a chatty letter about Washington, assuring you that I am well, and asking you kindly to consider the enclosed tabulated bill of expenses, as I need the money to buy Christmas presents and get home with.

Poker is one of the curses of national legislation. I have several times heard prominent foreigners say, in their own language—think ing, no doubt, that I could not understand them—that the members of the American Congress did not betray any emotion on their countenances. One foreigner from Liverpool, who thought I could not understand his language, said that our congressmen had a way of looking as though they did not know very much. When he afterwards played poker with those same men he saw that the look was acquired. One man told me that his vacant look had been as good as $50,000 to him, whether he stood pat or drew to an ostensible flush while really holding four bullets.

So far I have not been over to the Capitol, preferring to have Congress kind of percolate into my room, two or three at a time; but unless you can honor the inclosed way-bill I shall be forced to go over to the House to-morrow and write something for the paper. Since I have been writing this I have been led to inquire whether it would be advisable for me to remain here through the entire session or not. It will be unusually long, lasting perhaps clear into July, and I find that the stenographers as a general thing get a pretty accurate and spicey account of the proceedings, much more so than I can, and as you will see by inclosed statement it is going to cost more to keep me here than I figured on.

My idea was that board and lodgings would be the main items of expense, but I struck a low-priced place, where, by clubbing together with some plain gentlemen from a distance who have been waiting here three years for political recognition, and who do not feel like surrounding themselves with a hotel, we get a plain room with six beds in it. The room overlooks, the District of Columbia, and the first man in has the choice of beds, with the privilege of inviting friends to a limited number. We lunch plainly in the lower part of the building in a standing position without restraint or finger-bowls. So board is not the principal item of expense, though of course I do not wish to put up at a place where I will be a disgrace to the paper.

I wish that you would, when you send my check, write me frankly whether you think I had better remain here during the entire season or not. I like the place first rate, but my duties keep me up nights to a late hour, and I cannot sleep during the day, because my roommates annoy me by doing their washing and ironing over an oil stove.

I know by what several friends have said to me that Congress would like to have me stay here all winter, but I want to do what is best for the paper.

I saw Mr. Cleveland briefly last evening at his home, but he was surrounded by a crowd of fawning sycophants, so I did not get a chance to speak to him as I would like to, and don't know as he would have advanced the amount to me anyway. He is very firm and stubborn, I judged, and would yield very little indeed, especially to

Yours truly,

Bill Nye.

The following bill looks large in the aggregate, but when you come to examine each item by itself there is really nothing startling about it, and when you remember that I have been here now four days and that this is the first bill I have sent in to the office during that time, I know you will not consider it out of the way, especially as you are interested in seeing me make a good paper of the *World*, no matter what the expense is.

We are having good open winter weather and stock is looking well so far.

I fear you will regard the item for embalming as exorbitant, and it is so, but I was compelled to pay that price, as the man had to be shipped a long distance, and I did not want to shock his friends too much when he met them at the depot.

To rent of dress suit for the purpose of seeing life
in Washington in the interest of the paper $4 50
To charges for dispersing turtle soup from lap of
same 1 00
To getting fur collar put on overcoat, in interest of
paper. 9 00
To amount loaned a gentleman who had lived in
Washington a long time and could make me a
social pet (I will return same to you in case he
pays it before I come back) 5 00
To lodgings two nights at 25 cents 50
Six meals at 15 cents 90
Pen and ink 20
Postage on this letter 8
Bronchial troches, in interest of paper................. 20
Car fare 60
Laundry work done in interest of paper 30
Carriage hire in getting from humble home of a
senator to my own voluptuous lodgings 2 00
To expenses of embalming a man who came to me
and wanted me to use my influence in changing
policy of the paper 180 00
To fine paid for assault and battery in and upon a
gentleman who said he wanted my influence, but
really was already under other influence, and who
stepped on my stomach twice without offering to
apologize 19 00
Paid janitor of jail next morning...................... 1 00
Paid for breaking the window of my cell.............. 50
Paid damage for writing humorous poetry on wall
of cell so that it could not be erased................ 2 00

Total.. $226 18

I will probably remain here until I hear from you favorably. I have met several members of Congress for whom I have voted at various times off and on, but they were cold and haughty in their intercourse with me. I have been invited to sit on the floor of the House until I get some other place to stay, but I hate to ride a free horse to death.

b. n.

A PATENT ORATORICAL STEAM ORGANETTE FOR RAILWAY STUMPING

I AM now preparing for general use and desire to call the attention of numerous readers to what I have nominated the Campaigner's Companion, for use during or preceding a hot political campaign. Eureka is a very tame expression for this unique little contrivance, as it is good for any speaker and on behalf of any party, I care not of what political belief the orator may be. It is intended for immediate use, like a box of dry plates on an amateur photographic tour, only that it is more on the principle of the Organette, with from 500 to 5,000 tunes packed with it ready for use.

It is intended to be worked easily on the rear platform of a special car, and absolutely prevents repetition or the wrong application of local gags. Every political speaker of any importance has suffered more or less from what may be called the misplaced gag, such as localizing the grave of a well-known member of Congress in the wrong county or swelling up with pardonable pride over large soap works in a rival town fifty miles away from the one where they really are. All these things weaken the political possibilities of great men and bring contumely upon the party they represent.

My idea is to arrange a sort of Organette on the rear platform of the car, to be operated by steam conducted from the engine by means of pipes, the contrivance to be entirely out of sight, under a neat little spread made of the American flag. Behind this an eminent man may stand with his hand socked into the breast of his frock coat nearly up to the elbow, and while his bosom swells with pardonable pride the engineer turns on steam. Previously the private secretary has inserted a speech prepared on punched paper, furnished by me and bearing on that special town and showing a degree of familiarity with that neighborhood which would win the entire adult population.

Behind this machine the eminent speaker weaves to and fro, simply making the gestures and shutting off the steam with his foot whenever there is a manifest desire on the part of the audience to applaud.

I am having over five hundred good one-night towns prepared in this way and, if it would not take up too much of your space, I would like to give here one speech, illustrating my idea and showing the plan in brief, though with each machine I furnish a little book called "Every Man his Own Demosthenes." This book tells exactly how to work the Campaigner's Companion and makes it almost a pleasure to aspire to office.

I have chosen as an illustration a speech that I have had prepared for Asheville, N. C., but all the others are equally applicable and apropos.

(Note: See that all bearing's are well oiled before you start, especially political bearings. See that the crank is just tight enough, without being too tight, and also that the journals do not get hot.)

Fellow-Citizens of Asheville and Buncombe County and Brother Tarheels from Away Back:

If I were a faithful Mohammedan and believed that I could never enter heaven but once, I would look upon Buncombe County and despair ever afterwards. (Four minutes for applause to die away.) Asheville is 2,339 feet above tide-water. She is the hotbed of the invalid and the home of the physical wreck who cannot live elsewhere, but who comes here and lives till he gets plum sick of it. Your mountain breezes and your fried chicken bear strength and healing in their wings. (Hold valve open two minutes and a half to give laughter full scope.) Your altitude and your butter are both high, and the man who cannot get all the fresh air he wants on your mountains will do well to rent one of your cottages and allow the wind to meander through his whiskers. Asheville is a beautiful spot, where a peri could put in a highly enjoyable summer, picknicking along the Swananea through the day and conversing with Plum Levy at his blood-curdling barber shop in the gloaming. Nothing can possibly be thrillinger than to hear Plum tell of the hair-breadth escapes his customers have had in his cozy little shop.

The annual rainfall here is 40.2 inches, while smoking tobacco and horned cattle both do well. Ten miles away stretches Alexander's. You are only thirty-five miles from Buck Forest. Pisgah Mountain is only twenty miles from here, and Tahkeeastee Farm is only a mile away, with its name extending on beyond as far as the eye can reach. The French Broad River bathes your feet on the right and the sun-kissed Swananoa, with its beautiful borders of rhododendrons, sloshes up against you on the other side. Mount Mitchell, with an altitude of 6,711 feet and an annual rain-fall of 53.8 inches, is but twenty miles distant, while Lower Hominy is near, and Hell's Half Acre, Sandy Mush and Blue Ruin are within your grasp.

The sun never lit up a cuter little town than Asheville. Nature just seemed to wear herself out on Buncombe County and then she took what she had left over to make the rest of the country. Your air is full of vigor. Your farms get up and hump themselves in the middle or on one side, so that you have to wear a pair of telegraph-pole climbers when you dig your potatoes. Here you will see the japonica, the jonquil and the jaundice growing side by side in the spring, and at the cheese-foundry you can hear the skipper calling to his mate.

Here is the home of General Tom Clingman, who first originated the idea of using tobacco externally for burns, scalds, ringworm, spavin, pneumonia, Bright's disease, poll evil, pip, garget, heartburn, earache and financial stringency Here Randolph & Hunt can do your job printing for you, and the *Citizen* and the *Advance* will give you the news.

You are on a good line of railroad and I like your air very much, aside from the air just played by your home band. Certainly you have here the makings of a great city. You have pure air enough here for a city four times your present size, and although I have seen most all the Switzerlands of America, I think that this is in every way preferable. People who are in search of a Switzerland of America that can be relied upon will do well to try your town.

And now, having touched upon everything of national importance that I can think of, I will close by telling you a little anecdote which will, perhaps, illustrate my position better than I could do it in any other way. (Here I insert a humorous anecdote which has no special bearing on the political situation and during the ensuing laughter the train pulls out.)

VERITAS

MY NAME is Veritas. I write for the papers. I am quite an old man and have written my kindly words of advice to the press for many years. I am the friend of the public and the guiding star of the American newspaper. I point out the proper course for a newly-elected member of Congress and show the thoughtless editor the wants of the people. I write on the subject of political economy; also on both sides of the paper. Sometimes I write on both sides of the question. When I do so I write over the name of Tax-Payer, but my real name is Veritas.

I am the man who first suggested the culvert at the Jim street crossing, so that the water would run off toward the pound after a rain. With my ready pen—ready, and trenchant also, as I may say—I have, in my poor, weak way, suggested a great many things which might otherwise have remained for many years unsuggested.

I am the man who annually calls for a celebration of the Fourth of July in our little town, and asks for some young elocutionist to be selected by the committee, whose duty it shall be to read the Declaration of Independence in a shrill voice to those who yearn to be thrilled through and through with patriotism.

Did I not speak through the columns of the press in clarion tones for a proper observance of our nation's great natal day in large gothic extended caps, the nation's starry banner would remain furled and the greased pig would continue to crouch in his lair. With the aid of my genial co-workers Tax-Payer, Old Settler, Old Subscriber, Constant Reader, U. L. See, Fair Play, and Mr. Pro Bono Publico, I have made the world a far more desirable place in which to live than it would otherwise have been.

My co-laborer, Mr. Tax-Payer, is an old contributor to the paper, but he is not really a taxpayer. He uses this signature in order to conceal his identity, just as I use the name Veritas. We have a great deal of fun over this at our regular annual reunions, where we talk about all our affairs.

Old Settler is a young tenderfoot who came here last spring and tried to obtain a livelihood by selling an indestructible lamp-chimney. He did well for several weeks by going to the different residences and throwing one of his glass chimneys on the floor with considerable force to show that it would not break. He did a good business till one day he made a mistake. Instead of getting hold of his exhibition chimney, he picked out one of the stock and busted it beyond recognition. Since that he has been writing articles in violet ink relative to old times and publishing them over the signature of Old Settler.

Old Subscriber is a friend of mine who reads his paper at the hotels while waiting for a gratuitous drink. Fair Play is a retired monte man, and Pro Bono Publico is our genial and urbane undertaker.

I am a very prolific writer, but all my work is not printed. A venal and corrupt press at times hesitates about giving currency to such fearless, earnest truths as I make use of.

I am also the man who says brave things in the columns of the papers when the editor himself does not dare to say them because he is afraid he will be killed. But what recks Veritas the bold and free? Does he flinch or quail? Not a flinch; not a quail.

Boldly he flings aside his base fears, and with bitter vituperation he assails those he dislikes, and attacks with resounding blows his own personal enemies, fearlessly signing his name, Veritas, to the article, so that those who yearn to kill him may know just who he is.

What would the world do without Veritas? In the hands of a horde of journalists who have nothing to do but attend to their business, left with no anonymous friend to whom they can fly when momentous occasions arise, when the sound advice and better judgment of an outside friend is needed, their condition would indeed be a pitiable one. But he will never desert us. He is ever at hand, prompt to say, over his nom de plume, what he might hesitate to say over his own name, for fear that he might go home with a battle of Gettysburg under each eye and a nose like a volcanic eruption. He cheerfully attacks everything and everybody, and then goes away till the fight, the funeral, and the libel suit are over. Then he returns and assails the grim monster Wrong. He proposes improvements, and the following week a bitter reply comes from Tax-Payer. Pro Bono Publico, the retired three-card-monteist, says: "Let us have the proposed improvement, regardless of cost."

Then the cynical U. L. See (who is really the janitor at the blind asylum) grumbles about useless expense, and finally draws out from the teeming brain of Constant Reader a long, flabby essay, written on red-ruled leaves, cut out of an old meat-market ledger, written economically on both sides with light blue ink made of bluing and cold tea. This essay introduces, under the most trying circumstances, such crude yet original literary gems as:

Wad some power the giftie gie us, etc.

He also says:

The wee sma' hours ayant the twal.

And farther on:

Breathes there a man with soul so deal.

Who never to himself hath said, etc.

His essay is not so much the vehicle of thought as it is the accommodation train for fragments of his old school declamations to ride on.

But to Veritas we owe much. I say this because I know what I am talking about, for am I not old Veritas himself? Haven't I been writing things for the papers ever since papers were published? Am I not the man who for years has been a stranger to fear? Have I not again and again called the congressman, the capitalist, the clergyman, the voter and the philanthropist everything I could lay my tongue to, and then fought mosquitoes in the deep recesses of the swamp while the editor remained at the office and took the credit for writing what I had given him for nothing? Has not many a paper built up a name and a libel suit upon what I have written, and yet I am almost unknown? When people ask, Who is Veritas? and where does he live? no one seems to know. He is up seven flights of stairs, in a hot room that smells of old clothes and neglected thoughts. Far from the "madding crowd," as Constant Reader has so truly said, I sit alone, with no personal property but an overworked costume, a strong love for truth, and a shawl-strap full of suggestions to the overestimated man who edits the paper..

So I battle on, with only the meager and flea-bitten reward of seeing my name in print "anon," as Constant Reader would say. All I have to fork over to posterity is my good name, which I beg leave to sign here.

Veritas.

THE DRUG BUSINESS IN KANSAS

Hudson, Wis.

MR. BILL NYE.—Dear Sir: I hope you will pardon me for addressing you on a matter of pure business, but I have heard that you are not averse to going out of your way to do a favor now and then to those who are sincere and appreciative.

I have learned from a friend that you have been around all over the west, and so I have taken the liberty of writing you to ask what you think would be the chance of success for a young man if he were to go to Kansas to enter the drug business.

I am a practical young druggist 23 years of age, and have some money—a few hundred dollars—with which to go into business. Would you advise Kansas or Colorado as a good part of the west for that business?

I have also written some for the press, but with little success. I inclose you a few slips cut from the papers in which these articles originally appeared. I send stamp for reply and hope you will answer me, even though your time may be taken up pretty well by other matters. Respectfully yours.

Adolph Jaynes,

Lock-Box 604.

Hudson, Wis., Oct. 1.

MR. Adolph Jaynes, Lock-box 604.—

DEAR SIR: Your favor of late date is at hand, and I take pleasure in writing this dictated letter to you, using the columns of the Chicago Daily News as a delicate way of teaching you. I will take the liberty of replying to your last question first, if you pardon me, and I say that you would do better, no doubt at once, in a financial way, to go on with your drug business than to monkey with literature.

In the first place, your style of composition is like the present style of dress among men. It is absolutely correct, and therefore it is absolutely like that of nine men out of every ten we meet. Your style of writing has a mustache on it, wears a three-button cutaway of some Scotch mixture, carries a cane, and wears a straight, stand-up collar and scarf. It is so correct and so exactly in conformity with the prevailing style of composition, and your thoughts are expressed so thoroughly like other people's methods of dressing up their sentences and sand-papering the soul out of what they say, that I honestly think you would succeed better by trying to subsist upon the quick sales and small profits which the drug trade insures.

Now, let us consider the question of location.

Seriously, you ought to look over the ground yourself, but as you have asked me to give you my best judgment on the question of preference as between Kansas and Colorado I will say without hesitation that, if you mean by the drug business the sale of sure-enough drugs, medicines, paints, oils, glass, putty, toilet articles, and prescriptions carefully compounded, I would *not* go to Kansas at this time.

If you would like to go to a flourishing country and put out a big basswood mortar in front of your shop in order to sell the tincture of damnation throughout bleeding Kansas, now is your golden opportunity. Now is the accepted time.

If it is the great, big, burning desire of your heart to go into a town of 2,000 people and open the thirteenth drug store in order that you may stand behind a tall black-walnut prescription case day in and day out, with a graduate in one hand and a Babcock fire-extinguisher in the other, filling orders for whisky made of stump-water and the juice of future punishment, you will do well to go to Kansas. It is a temperance state, and no saloons are allowed there. All is quiet and orderly, and the drug business is a great success.

You can run a dummy drug store there with two dozen dreary old glass bottles on the shelves, punctuated by the hand of time and the Kansas fly of the period, and with a prohibitory law at your back and a tall, red barrel in the back room filled with a mixture that will burn great holes into nature's heart and make the cemetery blossom as the rose, and in a few years you can sell enough of this justly celebrated preparation for household, scientific, and experimental purposes only to fill your flabby pockets with wealth and paint the pure air of Kansas a bright and inflammatory red.

If you sincerely and earnestly yearn for a field where you may go forth and garner an honest harvest from the legitimate effort of an upright soda fountain and free and open sale of slippery elm in its unadulterated condition, I would go to some state where I would not have to enter into competition with a style of pharmacy that has the unholy instincts and ambitions of a blind pig. I would not go into the field where red-eyed ruin simply waited for a prescription blank, not necessarily for publication, but simply as a guaranty of good faith, in order that it may bound forth from behind the prescription case and populate the poorhouses and the paupers' nettle-grown addition to the silent city of the dead.

The great question of how best to down the demon rum is before the American people, and it will not be put aside until it is settled; but while this is being attended to, Mr. Jaynes, I would start a drug store farther away from the center of conflict and go on joyously, sacrificing expensive tinctures, compounds, and sirups at bed-rock prices.

Go on, Mr. Jaynes, dealing out to the yearning, panting public, drugs, paints, oils, glass putty, varnish, patent medicines, and prescriptions carefully compounded, with none to molest or make afraid, but shun, oh shun the wild-eyed pharmacopoeia that contains naught but the festering fluid so popular in Kansas, a compound that holds crime in solution and ruin in bulk, that shrivels up a man's gastric economy, and sears great ragged holes into his immortal soul. Take this advice home to your heart and you will ever command the hearty co-operation of "yours for health," as the late Lydia E. Pinkham so succinctly said.

THE PERILS OF IDENTIFICATION

Chicago, Feb. 20,1888.

FINANCIAL circles here have been a good deal interested in the discovery of a cipher which has been recently adopted by a depositor and which began to attract the attention at first of a gentleman employed in the Clearing House. He was telling me about it and showing me the vouchers or duplicates of them.

It was several months ago that he first noticed on the back of a check passing through the Clearing-House the following cipher, written in a symmetrical Gothic hand:

Dear Sir: Herewith find payment for last month's butter. It was hardly up to the average. Why do you blonde your butter? Your butter last month tried to assume an effeminate air, which certainly was not consistent with its vigor. Is it not possible that this butter is the brother to what we had the month previous, and that it was exchanged for its sister by mistake? We have generally liked your butter very much, but we will have to deal elsewhere if you are going to encourage it in wearing a full beard. Yours truly, W.

Moneyed men all over Chicago and financial cryptogrammers came to read the curious thing and to try and work out its bearing on trade. Everybody took a look at it, and went away defeated. Even the men who were engaged in trying to figure out the identity of the Snell murderer took a day off and tried their Waterbury thinkers on this problem. In the midst of it all another check passed through the Clearing House with this cipher, in the same hand:

Sir: Your bill for the past month is too much. You forget the eggs returned at the end of second week, for which you were to give me credit. The cook broke one of them by mistake, and then threw up the portfolio of pie-founder in our once joyous home. I will not dock you for loss of cook, but I cannot allow you for the eggs. How you succeed in dodging quarantine with eggs like that is a mystery to yours truly, W.

Great excitement followed the discovery of this indorsement on a check for $32.87. Everybody who knew anything about-ciphering was called in to consider it. A young man from a high school near here, who made a specialty of mathematics and pimples, and who could readily tell how long a shadow a nine pound groundhog would cast at 2 o'clock and 37 minutes p.m., on groundhog day, if sunny, at the town of Fungus, Dak., provided latitude and longitude and an irregular mass of red chalk be given to him, was secured to jerk a few logarithms in the interests of trade. He came and tried it for a few days, covered the interior of the Exposition Building with figures and then went away.

The Pinkerton detectives laid aside their literary work on the great train book, entitled "The Jerk-water Bank Bobbery and Other Choice Crimes," by the author of "How I Traced a Lame Man Through Michigan, and Other Felonies." They grappled with the cipher, and several of them leaned up against something and thought for a long time, but they could make neither head nor tail to it. Ignatius Donnelly took a powerful dose of kumiss, and under its maddening influence sought to solve the great problem which threatened to engulf the nation's surplus. All was in vain. Cowed and defeated, the able conservators of coin, who require a man to be identified before he can draw on his overshoes at sight, had to acknowledge if this thing continued it threatened the destruction of the entire national fabric.

About this time I was calling at the First National Bank of Chicago, the greatest bank, if I am not mistaken, in America. I saw the bonds securing its issue of national currency the other day in Washington, and I am quite sure the custodian told me it was the greatest of any bank in the Union. Anyway, it was sufficient, so that I felt like doing my banking business there whenever it became handy to do so.

I asked for a certificate of deposit for $2,000, and had the money to pay for it, but I had to be identified. "Why," I said to the receiving teller, "surely you don't require a man to be identified when he deposits money, do you?"

"Yes, that's the idea."

"Well, isn't that a new twist on the crippled industries of this country?"

"No; that's our rule. Hurry up, please, and don't keep men waiting who have money and know how to do business."

"Well, I don't want to obstruct business, of course, but suppose, for instance, I get myself identified by a man I know and a man you know and a man who can leave his business and come here for the delirious joy of identifying me, and you admit that I am the man I claim to be, corresponding as to description, age, sex, etc., with the man I advertise myself to be, how would it be about your ability to identify yourself as the man you claim to be? I go all over Chicago, visiting all the large pork-packing houses in search of a man I know, and who is intimate with literary people like me, and finally we will say, I find one who knows me and who knows you, and whom you know, and who can leave his leaf lard long enough to come here and identify me all right. Can you identify yourself in such a way that when I put in my $2,000 you will not loan it upon insufficient security, as they did in Cincinnati the other day, as soon as I go out of town?"

"Oh, we don't care especially whether you trade here or not, so that you hurry up and let other people have a chance. Where you make a mistake is in trying to rehearse a piece here instead of going out to Lincoln Park or somewhere in a quiet part of the city. Our rules are that a man who makes a deposit here must be identified."

"All right. Do you know Queen Victoria?"

"No sir; I do not."

"Well, then, there is no use in disturbing her. Do you know any other of the crowned heads?"

"No sir."

"Well, then, do you know President Cleveland, or any of the Cabinet, or the Senate or members of the House?"

"No."

"That's it, you see. I move in one set and you in another. What respectable people do you know?"

"I'll have to ask you to stand aside, I guess, and give that string of people a chance. You have no right to take up my time in this way. The rules of the bank are inflexible. We must know who you are, even before we accept your deposit."

I then drew from my pocket a copy of the Sunday *World* which contained a voluptuous picture of myself. Removing my hat and making a court salaam by letting out four additional joints in my lithe and versatile limbs, I asked if any further identification would be necessary.

Hastily closing the door to the vault and jerking the combination, he said that would be satisfactory. I was then permitted to deposit in the bank.

I do not know why I should always be regarded with suspicion wherever I go. I do not present the appearance of a man who is steeped in crime, and yet when I put my trivial, little, two-gallon valise on the seat of a depot waiting-room a big man with a red mustache comes to me and hisses through his clenched teeth: "Take yer baggage off the seat!" It is so everywhere. I apologize for disturbing a ticket agent long enough to sell me a ticket, and he tries to jump through a little brass wicket and throttle me. Other men come in and say: "Give me a ticket for Bandoline, O., and be dam sudden about it, too," and they get their ticket and go aboard the car and get the best seat, while I am begging for the opportunity to buy a seat at full rates and then ride in the wood box. I believe that common courtesy and decency in America needs protection. Go into an hotel or a hotel, whichever suits the eyether and nyether reader of these lines, and the commercial man who travels for a big sausage-casing house in New York has the bridal chamber, while the meek and lowly minister of the Gospel gets a wall-pocket room with a cot, a slippery-elm towel, a cake of cast-iron soap, a disconnected bell, a view of the laundry, a tin roof and $4 a day.

But I digress. I was speaking of the bank check cipher. At the First National Bank I was shown another of these remarkable indorsements. It read as follows:

Dear Sir: This will be your pay for chickens and other fowls received up to the first of the present month. Time is working' wondrous changes in your chickens. They are not such chickens as we used to get of you before the war. They may be the same chickens, but oh! how changed by the lapse of time! How much more indestructible! How they have learned since then to defy the encroaching tooth of remorseless ages, or any other man! Why do you not have them tender like your squashes! I found a blue poker chip in your butter this week. What shall I credit myself for it? If you would try to work your butter more and your customers less it would be highly appreciated, especially by, yours truly, W.

Looking at the signature on the check itself, I found it to be that of Mrs. James Wexford, of this city. Knowing Mr. Wexford, a wealthy and influential publisher here, I asked him today if he knew anything about this matter. He said that all he knew about it was that his wife had a separate bank account, and had asked him several months ago what was the use of all the blank space on the back of a check, and why it couldn't be used for correspondence with the remittee. Mr. Wexford said he'd bet $500 that his wife had been using her checks that way, for he said he never knew of a woman who could possibly pay postage on a note, remittance or anything else unless every particle of the surface had been written over in a wild, delirious, three-story hand. Later on I found that he was right about it. His wife had been sassing the grocer and the butter-man on the back of her checks. Thus ended the great bank mystery.

I will close this letter with a little incident the story of which may not be so startling, but it is true. It is a story of child faith. Johnny Quinlan, of Evanston, has the most wonderful confidence in the efficacy of prayer, but he thinks that prayer does not succeed unless it is accompanied with considerable physical strength. He believes that adult prayer is a good thing, but doubts the efficacy of juvenile prayer.

He has wanted a Jersey cow for a good while, and tried prayer, but it didn't seem to get to the central office. Last year he went to a neighbor who is a Christian and believer in the efficacy of prayer, also the owner of a Jersey cow.

"Do you believe that prayer will bring me a yaller Jersey cow?" said Johnny.

"Why, yes, of course. Prayer will remove mountains; it will do anything.

"Well, then, suppose you give me the cow you've got and pray for another one."

A FATHER'S LETTER

MY DEAR SOX: We got your last letter some three days ago. It found us all moderately well though not very frisky. Your letters now days are getting quite pretty as regards penmanship. You are certainly going to develop into a fine penman your mother thinks. She says that if you improve as fast in your writing next year as you have last, you will soon be writing for the papers.

In my mind's eye I can see you there in your room practicing for a long time on a spiral spring which you make with your pen. I believe you call it the whole arm movement. I think you got the idea from me. You remember I used to have a whole arm movement that I introduced into our family along in the summer of '69. You was at that time trying to learn to swim. Once or twice the neighbors brought you home with your lungs full of river water and your ears full of coarse sand. We pumped you dry several times, but it did not wean you from the river, so I introduced the whole arm movement, one day and used it from that on in what you would call our curric kulum. It worked well.

Your letters are now very attractive from a scientific standpoint. The letters all have pretty little curly tails on them, and though you do not always spell according to Gunter, the capital letters are as pretty as a picture. I never saw such a round O as you make when you hang your tongue out and begin to swing yourself. Your mother says that your great-uncle on her side was a good writer too. He could draw off a turtle dove without taking his pen from the paper, and most everybody would know as soon as they looked at it that it was a turtle dove or some such bird as that.

He could also draw a deer with coil spring horns on him, and a barbed wire fence to it, and a scolloped tail, and it looked as much like a deer as anything else you could think of.

He was a fine penman and wrote a good deal for the papers. Your mother has got a lot of his pieces in the house yet, which the papers sent back because they were busy and crowded full of other stuff. I read some of these letters, and any one can see that it was a great sacrifice for the editors to send the pieces back, but they had got used to it and conquered their own personal feelings, and sent them back because they were too good for the plain, untutored reader. One editor said that he did not want to print the enclosed pieces because he thought it would be a pity to place such pretty writing in the soiled hands of the practical printer. He said that the manuscript looked so pretty just as it was, that he hadn't the heart to send it into the composing room. So the day may not be far away, Henry, when you can write for the press, your mother thinks. I don't care so much about it myself, but she has her heart set on it. Your mother thinks that you are a great man, though I have not detected any symptoms of it yet. She has got that last pen scroll work here of yours in the bible, where she can look at it every day. Its the picture of a hen setting in a nest of curly-cues made with red ink, over a woven wire mattress of dewdads in blue ink, and some tall grass in violet ink. Your mother says that this fowl is also a turtle dove, but I think she is wrong.

She says the world has always got a warm place for one who can make such a beautiful picture without taking his pen off the paper. Perhaps she is right. I hope that you will not take me for an example, for I am no writer at all. My parents couldn't give me any advantages when I was young. When I ought to have been learning how to make a red ink bird of paradise swooping down on a violet ink butterfly with green horns, I was frittering away my time trying to keep my misguided parents out of the poor-house.

I tell you, Henry, there was mighty little fluff and bloom and funny business in my young life. While you are acquiring the rudiments of Long Dennis and polo and penmanship, and storing your mind with useful knowledge with which to parlize your poor parents when you come home, do not forget, Henry, that your old sway-back father never had those opportunities for soaking his system full of useful knowledge which you now enjoy. When I was your age, I was helping to jerk the smutty logs off of a new farm with a pair of red and restless steers, in the interest of your grandfather.

But, I do not repine. I just simply call your attention to your priviledges. Could you have a Summer in the heart of the primeval forest, thrown in contact with a pair of high-strung steers and a large number of black flies of the most malignant type, "snaking" half-burnt logs across yourself and fighting flies from early dawn till set of sun, you would be willing, nay tickled, to go back to your monotonous round of base ball and Suffolk jackets and pest-house cigarettes. .

We rather expected you home some time ago, but you said you needed sea air and change of scene, so you will not be home very likely till the latter part of the month. We will be glad to see you any time, Henry, and we will try to make it as pleasant as we can for you. Your mother got me to fill the big straw-tick for your bed again, so that you would have a nice tall place to sleep, and so that you could live high, as the feller said.

I tried on the old velocipede pants you sent home last week. They are too short for me with the style of legs I am using this Summer. Your bathing pants are also too short for me, so I gave them to a poor woman here who is trying to ameliorate the condition of her sex.

I send you our love and $9 in money. We will sell the other calf as soon as it is ripe. Chintz bugs are rather more robust than last year, and the mortgage on our place looks as if it might mature prematurely. We had a lecture on phrenology at the school-house Tuesday night, during which four of our this spring's roan turkies wandered so far away from home that they lost their bearings and never came back again. So good-by for this time. Your father,

Bill Nye

THE AZTEC AT HOME

IT HAS been my good fortune within the past ten years to witness a number of the remaining landmarks left to indicate the trail of the original inhabitant of this country. It has been a pleasure, and yet a kind of sad pleasure, to examine the crumbling ruins of what was once regarded, no doubt, as the very triumph of aboriginal taste and mechanical ingenuity.

I can take but a cursory glance at these earmarks of a forgotten age, for a short treatise like this cannot embrace minute details, of course.

We are told by the historian that there were originally two distinct classes of Indians occupying the territory now embraced by the United States, viz., the village Indians or horticultural Indians, and the extremely rural Indians or nonhorticultural variety.

The village Indians or horticulturalists subsisted upon fruits and grain, ground in a crude way, while the non-horticulturalists lived on wild game, berries, acorns and pilgrims.

Of the latter class few traces remain, excepting rude arrow heads and coarse stone weapons. These articles show very little skill as a rule, the only indication of brains that I ever discovered being on a large stone hammer or Mohawk swatter, and they were not the brains of the man who made it either.

The village Indians, however, were architects from away up the gulch.

They constructed a number of architectural works of great beauty, several of which I have visited. They were once, no doubt, regarded as very desirable residences, but now, alas, they have fallen into innocuous desuetude—at least that is what it looked like to me, and the odor reminded me of innocuous desuetude in a bad state of preservation.

In New Mexico, over 300 years ago, there were built a number of pereblos or villages which still stand up, in a measure, though some of them are in a recumbent position. These pereblos or villages are formed of three or four buildings constructed in the retrousse style of architecture, and made of adobe bricks. These bricks are generally of a beautiful, soft, black and tan color, and at a distance look like the first loaf of bread baked by a young lady who has been reared in luxury but whose father has been suddenly called away to Canada. The adobe brick is said to be so indigestible, in fact, that I am confident the day is not far distant when it will be found on every hotel bill of fare in our broad sin-cursed land.

One of these dwellings was generally about 200 feet long, with no stairways in the interior, but movable ladders on the outside instead. This manner of reaching the upper floor had its advantages, and yet it was not always convenient. One feature in its favor was the isolation which a man could pull around himself by going in at the second-story window and pulling the ladder up after him, as there was no entrance to the house on the ground floor. If a man really courted retirement, and wanted to write a humorous lecture or a $2 homily, he could insert himself through the second-story window, pull in the staircase and go to work. Then no one could disturb him without bribing a hook and ladder company to come along and let him in.

But the great drawback was the annoyance incident to ascending these ladders at a late hour in the night, while under the influence of Aztec rum, a very seductive yet violently intoxicating beverage, containing about eight parts cheer to ninety-two parts inebriate.

These residences were hardly gothic in style, being extremely rectangular, with a tendency toward the more modern dry-goods box. It is believed by abler men than I am, men who could believe more in two minutes than I could believe in a lifetime if I had nothing else to do, that those houses contained about thirty-eight apartments on the first floor and nineteen on the second. These apartments were separated by some kind of cheap and transitory partition, which could not stand the climatic changes, and so has gone to decay; but these Indians were determined to have their rooms separated in some way, for they were very polite and decorous to a fault. No Aztec gentleman would emerge from his room until he had completed his toilet, if it cost him his position.

I once heard of an Aztec who lived away down in old Mexico somewhere several centuries ago and who was the pink of politeness. He wore full-dress winter and summer, the whole year round, and studied a large work on etiquette every evening. At night he would undress himself by unhooking the german-silver ring from his nose and hanging it on the back of a chair.

One night a young man from the capital, named Ozone, or something like that, a relative of the Montezumas, came over to stay a week or two with this Aztec dude. As a good joke he slipped in and nipped the nose-ring of his friend just to see if he would so far violate the proprieties as to appear at breakfast time without it.

Morning came and the dude awoke to find the bright rays of a Mexican sun streaming in through his casement. He rose, and, bathing himself in a gourd, he looked on the back of the chair for his clothing, but it was not there. A cold perspiration broke out all over him. He called for assistance, but no one came. He called again and again, louder and still more loud, but help came not. He went to the casement and looked out upon the plaza. The plaza did not turn away. A Mexican plaza is not easily dashed.

He called till he was hoarse, but all was still in the house. Hollow echoes alone came back to him to mock him.

At night, when the rest of the household returned from a protracted picnic in the distant hills, young Ozone ascended the ladder which he carried with him in a shawl-strap, and entering the room of the Aztec dude gave him the nosering with a hearty laugh, but, alas! he was greeted with the wild, piercing shriek of a maniac robbed of his clothing; the man had suffered such mental tortures during the long, long day, that when night came, reason tottered on her throne. It is said that he never regained his faculties, but would always greet his visitors with a wild forty-cent shriek and bury his face in his hands. His friends tried to get him into society again, but he could not be prevailed upon to go. He seemed to be afraid that he would be shocked in some way, or that some one might take advantage of him and read an immoral poem to him.

IN THE SOUTH

ASHEVILLE, N.C., December 9.—There is no place in the United States, so far as I know, where the cow is more versatile or ambidextrous, if I may be allowed the use of a term that is far above my station in life, than here in the mountains of North Carolina, where the obese 'possum and the anonymous distiller have their homes.

Not only is the Tar-heel cow the author of a pale but athletic style of butter, but in her leisure hours she aids in tilling the perpendicular farm on the hillside, or draws the products to market. In this way she contrives to put in her time to the best advantage, and when she dies, it casts a gloom over the community in which she has resided.

The life of a North Carolina cow is indeed fraught with various changes and saturated with a zeal which is praiseworthy in the extreme. From the sunny days when she gambols through the beautiful valleys, inserting her black, retrousse and perspiration-dotted nose in to the blue grass from ear to ear, until at life's close, when every part and portion of her overworked system is turned into food, raiment or overcoat buttons, the life of the Tar-heel cow is one of intense activity.

Her girlhood is short, and almost before we have deemed her emancipated from calfhood herself we find her in the capacity of a mother. With the cares of maternity other demands are quickly made upon her. She is obliged to ostracize herself from society, and enter into the prosaic details of producing small, pallid globules of butter, the very pallor of which so thoroughly belies its lusty strength.

The butter she turns out rapidly until it begins to be worth something, when she suddenly suspends publication and begins to haul wood to market. In this great work she is assisted by the pearl-gray or ecru colored jackass of the tepid South. This animal has been referred to in the newspapers throughout the country, and yet he never ceases to be an object of the greatest interest.

Jackasses in the South are of two kinds, viz., male and female. Much as has been said of the jackass pro and con, I do not remember ever to have seen the above statement in print before, and yet it is as trite as it is incontrovertible. In the Rocky mountains we call this animal the burro.

There he packs bacon, flour and salt to the miners. The miners eat the bacon and flour, and with the salt they are enabled to successfully salt the mines.

The burro has a low, contralto voice which ought to have some machine oil on it. The voice of this animal is not unpleasant if he would pull some of the pathos out of it and make it more joyous.

Here the jackass at times becomes a coworker with the cow in hauling tobacco and other necessaries of life into town, but he goes no further in the matter of assistance. He compels her to tread the cheese press alone and contributes nothing whatever in the way of assistance for the butter industry.

The North Carolina cow is frequently seen here driven double or single by means of a small rope line attached to a tall, emaciated gentleman, who is generally clothed with the divine right of suffrage, to which he adds a small pair of ear-bobs during the holidays.

The cow is attached to each shaft and a small singletree, or swingletree, by means of a broad strap harness. She also wears a breeching, in which respect she frequently has the advantage of her escort.

I think I have never witnessed a sadder sight than that of a new milch cow, torn away from home and friends and kindred dear, descending a steep, mountain road at a rapid rate and striving in her poor, weak manner to keep out of the way of a small Jackson democratic wagon loaded with a big hogshead full of tobacco. It seems to me so totally foreign to the nature of the cow to enter into the tobacco traffic, a line of business for which she can have no sympathy and in which she certainly can feel very little interest.

Tobacco of the very finest kind is produced here, and is used mainly for smoking purposes. It is the highest-priced tobacco produced in this country. A tobacco broker here yesterday showed me a large quantity of what he called export tobacco. It looks very much like other tobacco while growing.

He says that foreigners use a great deal of this kind. I am learning all about the Tobacco industry while here, and as fast as I get hold of any new facts I will communicate them to the press. The newspapers of this country have done much for me, not only by publishing many pleasant things about me, but by refraining from publishing other things about me, and so I am glad to be able, now and then, to repay this kindness by furnishing information and facts for which I have no use myself, but which may be of incalculable value to the press.

As I write these lines I am informed that the snow is twenty-six inches deep here and four feet deep at High Point in this State. People who did not bring in their pomegranates last evening are bitterly bewailing their thoughtlessness to-day.

A great many people come here from various parts of the world, for the climate. When they have remained here for one winter, however, they decide to leave it where it is.

It is said that the climate here is very much like that of Turin. But I did not intend to go to Turin even before I heard about that.

Please send my paper to the same address, and if some one who knows a good remedy for chilblains will contribute it to the Sabbath Globe, I shall watch for it with great interest. Yours as here 2 4.

Bill N ye.

P.S.—I should have said relative to the cows of this State that if the owners would work their butter more and their cows less, they would confer a great boon on the consumer of both. B. N.

IN THE PARK

TO the general public I may say that I violate no confidence in saying that spring is the most joyful season of the year. But June is also a good month. Well has the poet ejaculated, "And what is so rare as a day in June?" though I have seen days in March that were so rare that they were almost raw. This is not a weather report; however. I started out to state that Central Park just now is looking its very best, and opens up with the prospects of doing a good business this season. A ride through the Park just now is a delight to one who loves to commune with nature, especially human nature.

The nobility of New York now turns out to get the glorious air and ventilate its crest. I saw several hundred crests and coats-of-arms the other day in an hour's time, and it was rather a poor day, too, for a great many of our best people are just changing from their spring to their light, summer coats-of-arms.

One of the best crests I saw was a nice, large, red crest, about the size of an adult rhubarb pie, with a two-year-old Durham unicorn above it, bearing in his talons the unique maxim, "*Sans culottes, sans snockemonthegob, sans ery sipelas est.*"

And how true this is, too, in a great many cases.

Another very handsome crest on the carriage of the van Studentickels consisted of a towel-rack penchant, with cockroach regardant, holding in his beak a large red tape-worm on which was inscribed: "*Spirituous frumenti, cum homo to-morrow.*"

Many of the crests contained terse Latin mottoes, taken from the inscriptions on peppermint conversation candies, and were quite cute. A coat-of-arms, consisting of a small Limburger cheese couchant, above which stood a large can of chloride of potash, on which was inscribed the words, "Miss, may I see you home?" I thought very taking and just mysterious enough to make it exciting.

Some day I am going to get myself a crest. I am only waiting for something to put it on. It will consist of a monkey with his eye knocked out and a bright green parrot with his tail pulled off, and over this the simple remark: "We have had a high old time," or words to that effect.

Not so many equestrians were out as usual on the day I visited the park, but those who were out afforded the observer a beautiful view of the park between their persons and the saddle. The equestriennes were more numerous, and one or two especially were as beautiful as anything that nature ever turned out. One young woman, in a neat-fitting plug hat, looked to me like a peri. It has been a good while now since I saw a peri, but I have always heard them very highly spoken of, and I hope she will not be offended when she reads these lines and finds that I regard her in that light.

Carriage-horses are dressing about as they did last season, except that pon-pon tails are more worn, especially at the end. Neck-yokes are cut low this year so as to show the shoulders of the wearer, and horses in mourning wear their tails at half-mast.

The porous plastron is not in favor this year, but many horses who interfere are wearing life-preservers over the fetlock, and sometimes a small chest-protector of russet leather over the joint, according to the taste of the wearer.

Polka-dot or half-mourning dogs are much affected by people who are beginning to get the upper hand of their grief. Much taste is shown in the selection of dogs for the coming season, and many owners chain their coachman to the dog, so that if any one were to come and try to abduct the dog the coachman could bite him and drive him away. A good coachman to take care of a watch-dog is almost invaluable.

A custom of taking the butler along in the seat with the coachman is growing in favor for two reasons: First, it shows that you have a butler, and, second, you know that while he is out with you he is not putting paste in the place of your diamonds at home. So I had almost said that it paste to do this.

The automatic or jointless footman is still popular, and a young man who has a good turning-lathe leg and an air of impenetrable gloom can get a job most any time.

Many New York gentlemen who are fond of driving take their grooms out to Central Park every afternoon for an airing. This is a wise provision, for those who have associated much with grooms will agree with me that a little airing now and then is just what they need.

There ought to be a book of park etiquette printed soon, however, for the guidance of its patrons. In the first place, it should be considered.

Autre for a gentleman to hire a coupe by the hour in order to recover from alcoholic prostration, and then sleep up and down the drive with his feet out the window. It is not respectful, and besides that the blood is liable to all rush to his head.

Drunken cab-drivers, too, should not be permitted to drive in the park, for only a little while ago one of them is said to have fallen from his high perch and injured his crest.

A park policeman should be specially detailed as a breath tester to stand at each entrance and smell the breath of all drivers and other patrons of the park. Let us enforce the law.

But the most curious feature about the exhibition afternoon spin in the Park is the great prevalence of mourning symbols. Almost, if not quite, one-third of the carriages one meets is decorated with black in every possible way, till sometimes it looks like a runaway funeral procession.

Why people should come to Central Park to advertise their woe by means of long black mourning tassels at their horses' heads and a draped driver with broad bands of bombazine concealing the russet tops of his boots, sometimes dressed in black throughout, is more than I can understand.

The honest, earnest and genuine affection of a good woman for a worthy man, alive or dead, is too sacred to treat lightly and the love that survives the wreck and ruin of gathering years has inspired more than one man to deeds of daring whereby he has won everlasting renown, but the woe that is divided up among the servants and shared in by the horses is not in good taste, it is not in good order and there are flies on it.

It is like saying to the world come and see how I suffer. It is parading your sore toe in Central Park, where people with sore toes are not supposed to congregate. It is like a widow wailing her woe through the "Want" column of a healthy morning paper. It is, in effect, saying to Christendom, come and hear me snort and see me paw up the ground in my paroxysms of wild and uncontrollable anguish. My grief is of such a penetrating nature and of that searching variety that it has broken out at the barn, and even the horses that I bought two weeks after the funeral, with a part of the life insurance money, have gone into mourning, and the coachman who got here day before yesterday from Liverpool has tied himself up in black bombazine and takes special delight in advertising our sorrow.

I do not believe that it will always be popular to wear mourning for our friends unless we feel a little doubtful about where they went.

Black is offensive to the eye, offensive to the nose, and it makes your flesh crêpe to touch it. Will the proofreader please deal gently with the above joke and I will do as much for him sometime.

Henry Ward Beecher had the right idea of the way to treat death, and when at last it came his turn to die his home and his church both seemed to say: "The great preacher is gone, but there is nothing about the change that is sad."

There is something the matter with grief that works itself up into black rosettes and long black banners that sweep the ground and shut out the sky and look like despair and feel like the season-cracked back of a warty dragon.

But wealth has its little eccentricities and we must bear with them. But he alone is indeed rich who is content and who does not look under the bed every night for an indictment. Look at poor old Mr. Sharp, with his stock of Aldermen depreciating on his hands—men for whom he paid a big price only a few years ago and who would not attract attention now on a ten-cent counter, while he don't feel very well himself.

No, I would not swap places with J. Sharp and ride through Central Park behind a pair of rip, snorting horses, with mourning rosettes on their heads, and feel that I must hurry back to help select an unprejudiced jury. I would rather hang on to the brow of a Broadway car till I got to Fifty-second street, and then stroll over to the menagerie and feed red pepper to the Sacred Cow and have a good, plain, quiet time than to wear fine clothes and be wealthy and hate myself all the time. I believe that I am happier in my untroubled, dreamless sleep on my quiet couch, which draws a salary during the daytime as an upright piano; happier browsing about at a different restaurant each day, so that the waiters will not get well acquainted with me and expect me to give them the money that I am saving up to go to Europe with; happier, I say, to be thus tossed about on the bosom of the great, heaving human tide than to have forty or fifty millions of dollars concealed about my person that I cannot remember how I obtained.

I dislike notoriety, and nothing irritates me more than the coarse curiosity of people who ride at night in the elevated trains and peer idly into my room as I toil over my sewing or go gayly about humming a simple air as I prepare the evening meal over my cute little portable oil stove, and though I have not courted this interest on the part of the people, and though I would prefer to live less in the eye of the public, I feel that, occupying the position I do, I cannot expect to wholly consult my own wishes in the matter, and I am content to live quietly and enjoy good health rather than wear good clothes and feel rocky all the time.

I would rather have a healthy alimentary

Than he garnished all over with passementerie.

LIBERTY ENLIGHTENING THE WORLD

WHEN Patrick Henry put his old cast-iron spectacles on the top of his head and whooped for liberty, he did not know that some day we would have more of it than we knew what to do with. He little dreamed that the time would come when we would have more liberty than we could pay for. When Mr. Henry sawed the air and shouted for liberty or death, I do not believe that he knew the time would one day come when Liberty would stand knee deep in the mud of Bedloe's Island and yearn for a solid place to stand upon.

It seems to me that we have too much liberty in this country in some ways. We have more liberty than we have money. We guarantee that every man in America shall fill himself up full of liberty at our expense, and the less of an American he is the more liberty he can have. If he desires to enjoy himself, all he needs is a slight foreign accent and a willingness to mix up with politics as soon as he can get his baggage off the steamer. The more I study American institutions the more I regret that I was not born a foreigner, so that I could have something to say about the management of our great land. If I could not be a foreigner, I believe I would prefer to be a Mormon or an Indian not taxed.

I am often led to ask, in the language of the poet, "Is the Caucasian played out?" Most everybody can have a good deal of fun in this country except the American. He seems to be so busy paying his taxes all the time that he has very little time to mingle in the giddy whirl with the alien. That is the reason that the alien who rides across the United States on the "Limited Mail" and writes a book about us before breakfast wonders why we are always in a hurry. That is the reason we have to throw our meals into ourselves with a dull thud, and hardly have time to maintain a warm personal friendship with our families.

We do not care much for wealth, but we must have freedom, and freedom costs money. We have advertised to furnish a bunch of freedom to every man, woman or child who comes to our shores, and we are going to deliver the good whether we have any left for ourselves or not.

What would the great world beyond the seas say to us if some day the blue-eyed Mormon, with his heart full of love for our female seminaries and our old women's homes, should land upon our coasts and find that we were using all the liberty ourselves? What do we want of liberty anyhow? What could we do with it if we had it? It takes a man of leisure to enjoy liberty, and we have no leisure whatever. It is a good thing to keep in the house "for the use of guests only," but we don't need it for ourselves.

Therefore, I am in favor of a statue of Liberty Enlightening the World, because it will show that we keep it on tap winter and summer. We want the whole broad world to remember that when it gets tired of oppression it can come here to America and oppress us. We are used to it, and we rather like it. If we don't like it, we can get on the steamer and go abroad, where we may visit the effete monarchies and have a high old time.

The sight of the Goddess of Liberty standing there in New York harbor night and day, bathing her feet in the rippling sea, will be a good thing. It will be first-rate. It may also be productive of good in a direction that many have not thought of. As she stands there day after day, bathing her feet in the broad Atlantic, perhaps some moss-grown Mormon moving toward the Far West, a confirmed victim of the matrimonial habit, may fix the bright picture in his so-called mind, and remembering how, on his arrival in New York, he saw Liberty bathing her feet with impunity, he may be led in after years to try it on himself.

HE SEES THE CAPITAL

WHEN I got off the Pennsylvania train yesterday I went to a barber shop before I did anything else. I have a thick, Venetian red, chinchilla beard, which grows rapidly, and which gives me a fuzzy appearance every twenty-four hours, unless I place myself frequently into the hands of a barber. At first I used to shave myself, but I cut myself to pieces in such a sickening manner, without seeming to impede the growth of the rich and foxy beard, that until last summer I gave up being my own barber. At that time I was presented with a safety razor which the manufacturer said would not cut my face, because it was impossible for it to cut anything except the beard. The safety razor resembles in appearance several other toilet articles, such as the spoke shave, the road scraper, the can opener, the lawn mower and the turbine water wheel, but it does not look like a razor. It also looks like a carpet sweeper some, and reminds me of a monkey wrench. It is said that you can shave yourself on a train if you will use this instrument. I tried it once last winter while going west. In fact, I took the trip largely to see if one could shave on board the train safely with this razor. I had no special trouble. At least I did not cut off any features that I cared anything about, but I was disappointed in the results, and also in the length of time consumed in cleaning the razor after I got through. I was shaving myself only from Forty-second street to Albany, but it took me from Albany to Omaha to pull the razor apart, and to dig out the coagulated lather and the dear, dear whiskers. I now employ a valet whose name is Patria McGloria. He irons my trousers, shaves and dresses me, and mows the lawn. When I come to Washington, I am too democratic to travel with a valet, fearing that it might cost me several thousand votes some day, and so I leave my maid at home to wash and dress the salad. In that way he does not miss me, and I get the credit at Washington of being a man who spends so much time thinking of his country's welfare that he doesn't have a chance to look pretty.

I did not fall into a very gaudy barber shop. The appointments were like some of the president's appointments, I thought—viz., in poor taste, but this is not a political letter. I do not wish to antagonize anybody, especially the president of the United States. He has always treated me well.

I will now return to the barber shop. It was a plain structure, with beautiful sarsaparilla pictures here and there on the walls and a faint odor of rancid pomatum and overworked hair restoratives.

There were three chairs richly upholstered in two-ply carpeting of some inflammatory hue, with large vines and the kind of flowers which grow on carpets but nowhere else. I have seen blossoms woven into ingrain carpets, varying in color from a dead black to the color of a hepatized lung, but I have never seen one that reminded me of anything I ever saw in nature. The chair I sat in also had springs in it. They were made of selections from the Washington monument.

The barber who waited on me asked me if I wanted a shave. A great many barbers ask me this during the year. Sometimes they do it from habit, and sometimes they do it to brighten up my life and bring a smile to my wan cheek. As I have no hair, the thinking mind naturally and by a direct course of reasoning arrives at the conclusion that when I go into a barber shop and climb into a chair, I do so for the purpose of getting shaved and not with the idea of having my fortune told or my deposition taken. Still barbers continue to ask me this question and look at each other with ill concealed mirth.

I said yes, I would like a shave unless he preferred to take my temperature, or amuse me by making a death mask of himself. He then began to strap a large razor with a double shuffle movement and to size me up at the same time.

He was a colored man, but he had lived in Washington a long time and knew a great deal more than he would if his lot had fallen elsewhere. He spoke with some feeling and fed me with about the most unpalatable lather I think I ever participated in. He also did an odd thing when he went for the second time over my face. I never have noticed the custom outside of that shop. Most barbers, in making the second trip over a customer's face, moisten one side at a time with a sponge or the damp hand as they go along, but in this case a large quantity of lather was put in my ear and, as he needed it, he took out what he required from time to time, using his finger like a paint brush and spreading on the lather as he went along. So accurately had he learned to measure the quantity of lather which an ear will hold that when he got through with me and I went away there was not over a tablespoonfnl in either ear and possibly not that much.

While I sat in the chair I heard a man, who seemed to be in about the third chair from me, saying that a certain bill numbered so-and-so had been referred to a certain committee and would undoubtedly by reported favorably. If so, it would in its regular order come up for discussion and reach a vote so-and-so. I was charmed with the man's knowledge of the condition of affairs in both houses and the exact status of all threatened legislation, because I always have to stop and think a good while before I can tell whether a bill originates on the floor of the house or in the rotunda.

I could not see this man, but I judged that he was a senator or sergeant-at-arms. He talked for some time about the condition of national affairs, and finally some one said something about evolution. I was perfectly wrapped up in what he was saying and remember distinctly how he referred to Herbert Spencer's definition of evolution as a change from indefinite, coherent heterogeneity through continuous differentiations and integrations.

When I arose from my chair and looked over that way I saw that the gentleman who had been talking on the condition of congressional legislation was a colored hotel porter of Washington, who was getting shaved in the third chair, and the man who was discussing the merits of evolution was the colored man who was shaving him.

Here in Washington the colored man has the air of one who is holding up one corner of the great national structure. Whether he is opening your soft boiled eggs for you in the morning, or putting bay rum on your nose, or checking your umbrella or brushing you with a wilted whisk broom, his thoughts are mostly upon national affairs. He is naturally an imitator wherever he goes, and this old resident of Washington has watched and studied the air and language of eminent statesmen so carefully that when he goes forth in the morning with his whitewashing portfolio on his arm he walks unconsciously like Senator Evarts or John James Ingalls. I saw a colored man taking a perpendicular lunch at the depot yesterday, and evidently the veteran Georgia senator is his model, for he cut his custard pie into large rectangular hunks and pushed it back behind his glottis with a caseknife, after which he drew in a saucerful of tea, with a loud and violent ways-and-means committee report which reminded me of the noise made by an unwearied cyclone trying to suck a cistern dry. I think that the colored man exaggerated the imitation somewhat, but he was evidently trying to assume the table manners of Senator Brown of Georgia.

For this reason, if for no other, members of the cabinet, senators, representatives, judges and heads of departments cannot be too careful in their daily walk and conversation. Unconsciously they are molding the customs, the manners, and the styles of dress which are to become the customs, the manners, and the dress of a whole race. If I could to-day take our statesmen all apart, not so much for the purpose of examining their works, but so that we could be alone and talk this matter over by ourselves, I would strive in my poor, weak, faltering way to impress upon them the awful responsibility which rests upon them not only as polite and fluent conversationalists, classical and courteous debators. speaking pieces for the benefit of future conventions, of referring to each other as liars, traitors, thieves, deserters, bummers, beats, and great moral abscesses on the body politic; rehearsing campaign speeches in congress at an expense of $20 per day each, and meantime obstructing wholesome tariff legislation, but as the conservators of etiquette, statesmanship, and morality for a race of people the great responsibility for whose welfare still rests upon us as a nation.

Only the day before yesterday I saw a thin, wiry, and colored gentleman pawing around in an ash barrel for something, and I waited to see what he was after. He resurrected a sad and dejected plug hat, and, though it was not half so good as the one he wore, he seemed much pleased with it and put it on. I ventured to ask him why he had done so without improving his appearance, and he said that for a long time he had been looking for a hat which would highten the resemblance which people had often noticed and remarked in days gone by, both in person, sah, and general carriage, walk, and conversation, sah, also in the matter of clear cut and logical life sentences, as existing between himself, sah, and Senator Evarts, sah. He believed that he had struck it, sah.

As spring warms up the air about Washington the heating apparatus of the capitol building begins to relax its interest, and now you can visit most any part of the stately pile without being scrambled in your own embonpoint. Last winter I heard Senator Frye of Maine make his great tariff speech, and although there was nothing, about the speech itself which seemed to evolve much exercise or industry—for it was the same speech in every essential quality that I have heard every November since I began to take an interest in politics—the perspiration ran down his face in small washouts and sweatlets and fell in the arena with a mellow plunk.

I believe this unnatural heat to be the cause of much ill health among our law-makers, and I freely admit that the unhealthy surroundings of Washington and the great contrast between the hot air of the capitol and the cold air outside have done a great deal towards keeping me out of the senate. The night air of Washington is also filled with malaria and is much worse than any night air I have ever used before.

HE SEES THE NAVY

IT HAS become such a general practice to speak disrespectfully of the United States Navy that a few days ago I decided to visit the Brooklyn Navy Yard for the purpose of ascertaining, if possible, how much cause there might be for this light and airy manner of treating the navy, and, if necessary, to take immediate steps towards purifying the system.

I found that the matter had been grossly misrepresented, and that our navy, so far as I was able to discover, is self-sustaining. It has been thoroughly refitted and refurnished throughout, and is as pleasant a navy as one would see in a day's journey.

I had the pleasure of boarding the man-of-war Richmond under a flag of truce and the Atlantic under a suspension of the rules. I remained some time on board each of these war ships, and any man who speaks lightly of the United States Navy in my presence hereafter will receive a stinging rebuke.

The Brooklyn Navy Yard was inaugurated by the purchase of forty acres of ground in 1801. It has a pleasant water-front, which is at all times dotted here and there with new war vessels undergoing repairs. Since the original purchase others have been made and the land side of the yard inclosed by means of a large brick wall, so that in case there should be a local disturbance in Brooklyn the rioters could not break through and bite the navy. In this way a man on board the Atlanta while at anchor in Brooklyn is just as safe as he would be at home.

In order to enter and explore the Navy Yard it is necessary that one should have a pass. This is a safeguard, wisely adopted by the Commandant, in order to keep out strangers who might get in under the pretext of wishing to view the yard and afterwards attack one of the new vessels.

On the day I visited the Navy Yard just ahead of me a plain but dignified person in citizen's dress passed through the gate. He had the bearing of an officer, I thought, and kept his eye on some object about nine and one-fourth miles ahead as he walked past the guard. He was told to halt, but, of course, he did not do so.

He was above it. Then the guard overhauled him, and even felt in his pockets for his pass, as I supposed. Concealed on his person the guard found four pint bottles filled with the essence of crime. They poured the poor man's rum on the grass and then fired him out, accompanied by a rebuke which will make him more deliberate about sitting down for a week or two.

The feeling against arduous spirits in the United States Navy is certainly on the increase, and the day is not far distant when alcohol in a free state will only be used in the arts, sciences, music, literature and the drama.

The Richmond is a large but buoyant vessel painted black. It has a front stairway hanging over the balcony, and the latch-string to the front door was hanging cheerily out as we drew alongside. During an engagement, however, on the approach of the enemy, the front stairs are pulled up and the latch-string is pulled in, while the commanding officer makes the statement, "April Fool" through a speaking-trumpet to the chagrined and infuriated foe.

The Richmond is a veteran of the late war, a war which no one ever regretted more than I did; not so much because of the bloodshed and desolation it caused at the time, but on account of the rude remarks since made to those who did not believe in the war and whose feelings have been repeatedly hurt by reference to it since the war closed.

The guns of the Richmond are muzzle-loaders, *i.e.*, the load or charge of ammunition is put into the other or outer end of the gun instead of the inner extremity or base of the gun, as is the case with the breech-loader. The breech-loader is a great improvement on the old style gun, making warfare a constant source of delirious joy now, whereas in former times in case of a naval combat during a severe storm, the man who went outside the ship to load the gun, while it was raining, frequently contracted pneumonia.

Modern guns are made with breeches, which may be easily removed during a fight and replaced when visitors come on board. A sort of grim humor pervades the above remark.

The Richmond is about to sail away to China. I do not know why she is going to China but presume she does not care to be here during the amenities, antipathies and aspersions of a Presidential campaign. A man-of-war would rather make some sacrifices generally than to get into trouble.

I must here say that I would rather be captured by our naval officers than by any other naval officers I have ever seen. The older officers were calm and self-possessed during my visit on board both the Richmond and Atlanta, and the young fellows are as handsome as a steel engraving. While gazing on them as they proudly trod the quarter deck or any other deck that needed it, I was proud of my sex, and I could not help thinking that had I been an unprotected but beautiful girl, hostile to the United States, I could have picked out five or six young men there to either of whom I would be glad to talk over the details of an armistice. I could not help enjoying fully my hospitable treatment by the officers above referred to after having been only a little while before rudely repulsed and most cruelly snubbed by a haughty young cotton-sock broker in a New York store.

When will people ever learn that the way to have fun with me is to treat me for the time being as an equal?

It was wash-day on board ship, and I could not help noticing how the tyrant man asserts himself when he becomes sole boss of the household. The rule on board a man-of-war is that the first man who on wash-day shall suggest a "picked-up dinner" shall be loaded into the double-barrelled howitzer and shot into the bosom of Venus.

On the clothes-line I noticed very few frills. The lingerie on board a war vessel is severe in outline and almost harsh in detail. Here the salt breezes search in vain for the singularly sawed-off and fluently trimmed toga of our home life. Here all is changed. From the basement to the top of the lightning rod, from pit to dome, as I was about to say, a belligerent ship on washday is not gayly caparisoned.

The Atlanta is a fair representative of the modern war vessel and would be the most effective craft in the world if she could use her guns. She has all the modern improvements, hot and cold water, electric lights, handy to depots and a good view of the ocean, but when she shoots off her guns they pull out her circles, abrade her deck, concuss her rotunda, contuse the main brace and injure people who have always been friendly to the Government. Her guns are now being removed and new circles put in, so that in future she would be enabled to give less pain to her friends and squirt more gloom into the ranks of the enemy. She is at present as useful for purposes of defense as a revolver in the bottom of a locked-up bureau drawer, the key of which is in the pocket of your wife's dress in a dark closet, wherein also the burglar is, for the nonce, concealed.

Politics has very little to do with the conduct of a navy-yard. No one would talk politics with me. I could not arouse any interest there at all in the election. Every one seemed delighted with the present Administration, however. The navy-yard always feels that way.

In the choky or brig at the guard-house I saw a sailor locked up who was extremely drunk.

"How did you get it here, my man?" I asked.

"Through thinfloonee of prominent Democrat, you damphool. Howje spose?" he unto me straightway did reply.

The sailor is sometimes infested with a style of arid humor which asserts itself in the most unlooked-for fashion. I laughed heartily at his odd yet coarse repartee, and went away.

The guard-house contains a choice collection of manacles, handcuffs, lily irons and other rare gems. The lily irons are not now in use. They consist of two iron bands for the wrists, connected by means of a flat iron, which can be opened up to let the wrists into place; then they are both locked at one time by means of a wrench like the one used by a piano-tuner. With a pair of lily irons on the wrists and another pair on the ankles a man locked in the brig and caught out 2,000 miles at sea in a big gale, with the rudder knocked off the ship and a large litter of kittens in the steam cylinder, would feel almost helpless.

I had almost forgotten to mention the drug store on board ship. Each man-of-war has a small pharmacy on the second floor. It is open all night, and prescriptions are carefully compounded. Pure drugs, paints, oils, varnishes and putty are to be had there at all times. The ship's dispensary is not a large room, but two ordinary men and a truss would not feel crowded there. The druggists treated me well on board both ships, and offered me my choice of antiseptics and anodynes, or anything else I might take a fancy to. I shall do my trading in that line hereafter on board ship.

The Atlanta has many very modern improvements, and is said to be a wonderful sailor. She also has a log. I saw it. It does not look exactly like what I had, as an old lumberman, imagined that it would.

It is a book, with writing in it, about the size of the tax-roll for 1888. In the cupola of the ship, where the wheel is located, there is also a big brass compass about as large as the third stomach of a cow. In this there is a little index or dingus, which always points towards the north. That is all it has to do. On each side of the compass is a large cannon ball so magnetized or polarized or influenced as to overcome the attraction of the needle for some desirable portion of the ship. There is also an index connected with the shaft whereby the man at the wheel can ascertain the position of the shaft and also ascertain at night whether the ship is advancing or retreating—a thing that he should inform himself about at the earliest possible moment.

The culinary arrangements on board these ships would make many a hotel blush, and I have paid $1 a day for a worse room than the choky at the guard-house.

In the Navy-Yard at Brooklyn is the big iron hull or running gears of an old ship of some kind which the Republicans were in the habit of hammering on for a few weeks prior to election every four years. Four years ago, through an oversight, the workmen were not called off nor informed of Blaine's defeat for several days after the election..

The Democrats have an entirely different hull in another part of the yard on which they are hammering.

The keel blocks of a new cruiser, 375 feet long are just laid in the big ship-house at the Brooklyn Navy-Yard. She will be a very airy and cheerful boat, I judge, if the keel blocks are anything to go by.

In closing this account I desire to state that I hope I have avoided the inordinate use of marine terms, as I desire to make myself perfectly clear to the ordinary landsman, even at the expense of beauty and style of description. I would rather be thoroughly understood than confuse the reader while exerting myself to show my knowledge of terms. I also desire to express my thanks to the United States Navy for its kindness and consideration during my visit. I could have been easily blown into space half a dozen times without any opportunity to blow back through the papers, had the navy so desired, and yet nothing but terms of endearment passed between the navy and myself.

Lieut. Arthur P. Nazro, Chief Engineer Henry B. Nones, Passed Assistant Engineer E. A. Magee, Capt. F. H. Harrington, of the United States Marine Corps; Mr. Gus C. Roeder, Apothecary Henry Wimmer and the dog Zib, of the Richmond; Master Shipwright McGee, Capt. Miller, captain of the yard, and Mr. Milligan, apothecary of the Atlanta, deserve honorable mention for coolness and heroic endurance while I was there.

MORE ABOUT WASHINGTON

WASHINGTON, D.C. I Have just returned from a polite and recherche party here.

Washington is the hot-bed of gayety, and general headquarters for the recherche business. It would be hard to find a bontonger aggregation than the one I was just at, to use the words of a gentleman who was there, and who asked me if I wrote "The Heathen Chinee."

He was a very talented man, with a broad sweep of skull and a vague yearning for something more tangible—to drink. He was in Washington, he said, in the interests of Mingo county. I forgot to ask him where Mingo county might be. He took a great interest in me, and talked with me long after he really had anything to say. He was one of those fluent conversationalists frequently met with in society. He used one of these web-perfecting talkers—the kind that can be fed with raw Roman punch and that will turn out punctuated talk in links, like varnished sausages. Being a poor talker myself and rather more fluent as a listener, I did not interrupt him.

He said that he was sorry to notice how young girls and their parents came to Washington as they would to a matrimonial market.

I was sorry also to hear it. It pained me to know that young ladies should allow themselves to be bamboozled into matrimony. Why was it, I asked, that matrimony should ever single out the young and fair?

"Ah," said he, "it is indeed rough!"

He then breathed a sigh that shook the foliage of the speckled geranium near by, and killed an artificial caterpillar that hung on its branches.

"Matrimony is all right," said he, "if properly brought about. It breaks my heart, though, to notice how Washington is used as a matrimonial market. It seems to me almost as if these here young ladies were brought here like slaves and exposed for sale." I had noticed that they were somewhat exposed, but I did not know that they were for sale.

I asked him if the waists of party dresses had always been so sadly in the minority, and he said they had.

I danced with a beautiful young lady whose trail had evidently caught in a doorway. She hadn't noticed it till she had walked out partially through her costume. I do not think a lady ought to give too much thought to her apparel, neither should she feel too much above her clothes. I say this in the kindest spirit, because I believe that man should be a friend to woman. No family circle is complete without a woman. She is like a glad landscape to the weary eye. Individually and collectively, woman is a great adjunct of civilization and progress. The electric light is a good thing, but how pale and feeble it looks by the light of a good woman's eyes. The telephone is a great invention. It is a good thing to talk at and murmur into and deposit profanity in, but to take up a conversation and keep it up and follow a man out through the front door with it, the telephone has still much to learn from woman.

It is said that our government officials are not sufficiently paid, and I presume that is the case, so it became necessary to economize in every way, but, why should wives concentrate all their economy on the waist of a dress? When chest protectors are so cheap as they now are, I hate to see people suffer, and there is more real suffering, more privation and more destitution, pervading the Washington scapula and clavicle this winter than I ever saw before.

But I do not hope to change this custom, though I spoke to several ladies about it, and asked them to think it over. I do not think they will. It seems almost wicked to cut off the best part of a dress and put it at the other end of the skirt, to be trodden under feet of men, as I may say. They smiled good humoredly at me as I tried to impress my views upon them, but should I go there again next season and mingle in the mad whirl of Washington, where these fair women are also mingling in said mad whirl, I presume that I will find them clothed in the same gaslight waist, with trimmings of real vertebræ down the back.

Still, what does a man know about the proper costume for woman? He knows nothing whatever. He is in many ways a little inconsistent. Why does a man frown on a certain costume for his wife and admire it on the first woman he meets? Why does he fight shy of religion and Christianity and talk very freely about the church, but get mad if his wife is an infidel?

Crops around Washington are looking well. Winter wheat, crocusses and indefinite postponements were never in a more thrifty condition. Quite a number of people are here who are waiting to be confirmed. Judging from their habits, they are lingering around here in order to become confirmed drunkards.

I leave here to-morrow with a large, wet towel in my plug hat. Perhaps I should have said nothing on this dress reform question while my hat is fitting me so immediately. It is seldom that I step aside from the beaten path of rectitude, but last evening, on the way home, it seemed to me that I didn't do much else but step aside. At these parties no charge is made for punch. It is perfectly free. I asked a colored man who stood near the punch bowl, and who replenished it ever and anon, what the damage was, and he drew himself up to his full height.

Possibly I did wrong, but I hate to be a burden on any one. It seemed odd to me to go to a first-class dance and find the supper and the band and the rum all paid for. It must cost a good deal of money to run this government.

A GREAT BENEFACTOR

IT WAS not generally known at the time, but about a year ago a gentleman from Jays-burg, named Alanson G-. Meltz, opened a law office in Chicago, intending to give that city a style of clear-cut counseling, soliciting, conveyancing, prosecuting and defending, such as she had never witnessed before. He was young, but he was full of confidence, and as he pulled the nails out of the dry goods boxes, in which he had brought his revised statutes and replevin appliances, he felt ready and willing to furnish advice at living rates to all who would come and examine his stock.

But time kept on in his remorseless flight, bringing in at the casement of Mr. Meltz the roar and hum of traffic, and the nut-brown flavor of the Chicago river, but that was all. He was there, ready and almost eager to advise one and all, but one and all, without exception, evaded him. No matter how gayly he lettered his window with the announcement that he would procure a divorce for any one without pain, married people continued to suffer on or go elsewhere. Even though he had put up a transparency:

DIVORCES PREPARED

WHILE YOU WAIT!

No one called at his office, No. 61 Water street, to get one. Day after day innumerable people went by him in the mad rush and hurry of life, married but not mated, forgetting that Mr. Meltz could relieve them without publicity.

Remorseless time had rolled on in this way for three months, now and then picking out a fragment of the cornice on the new court-house and braining a pedestrian with it, when one day Mr. Meltz was solicited by the proprietor of a new remedy for indigestion and brain-fever to try his medicine. He also told Mr. Meltz that in case of cure or beneficial effects he desired to use his endorsement, and as the remedy was new he proposed to issue an edition of 1,000,000 circulars containing the endorsement of prominent professional people of Chicago.

Alanson G. Meltz bought a bottle and began using it. In three weeks the following endorsement entered over a million and a half families in the United States at the expense of the man who owned the remedy:

Chicago, Dec. 13, 1883.

Dr. J. Burdock Wells.—

Sir: I am a lawyer of this city, and for the past year have been seriously and dangerously afflicted with sharp, darting pains up and down the spinal column, dimness of sight, acidity of the tonsils and in-growing spleen. I suffered the agonies of the d———d.

I take this method of informing the world, especially those who may be suffering as I did, that less than a month ago I was in a pitiful state. I have a large practice, especially as an attorney, in procuring noiseless divorces. My office is at No. 6 5/8 South Water Street, and for years I have been engaged in this line, procuring divorces for thousands everywhere, orders filled by mail, etc., by a new system of my own, by which applicants throughout the union may be treated at a distance as well as in my office.

This had so taken up my time and engrossed my attention that, before I knew it, my health had become impaired materially, and I did not know at any time but that the next succeeding moment might be my subsequent one. With clients calling on me and pressing me by mail for their services, with persistent people hurrying and urging me for divorces, so that they could marry some one else without unnecessary delay, I was stricken down with ingrowing spleen and gastric yearning of the most violent character. My physicians gave me up. They said I could never recover. I was in despair.

At that moment, like a clap of thunder from a clear sky, came Dr. J. Burdock Wells, with a bottle of his unerring Bile Renovator and Gastric Rectifier. I took one bottle and called for another. In a little while I began to hope.

When I arose in the morning my mouth did not taste like that of a total stranger any more. In one week my eye had recovered its old brilliancy, and in ten days I was back in my office again at No. 6 5/8 South Water Street, rapidly catching up with my large business and answering all calls made upon me from all quarters. I have not only regained my health, but I have been the humble means, since my recovery, of bringing peace to many an aching heart. One man from Kansas writes me: "Your recovery was indeed a great boon to me. You have saved my life. Whenever I want a divorce again I shall surely go to you. God bless you and prolong your life for many years that you may go on spreading joy and hope again throughout our broad land, furnishing your automatic and delightful divorces to those who suffer." I can most heartily endorse Dr. J. Burdock Wells' remedy and would cheerfully recommend it to those who have tried everything else without success. I would be glad to have any or all who suffer call at my office, No.

6 5/8 South Water street, if they doubt my recovery, when they will find me removing superfluous husbands or wives absolutely without pain.

Alanson G. Meltz.

Attorney and counselor-at-law, solicitor in chancery.

Practices in all the courts. Divorces sent C. O. D. at a moment's notice. Try our home treatment for divorce.

A man who visited Mr. Meltz' office last week says that his business is simply enormous, and that he has added to his former office the gorgeous room at No. 7 1/8 People are now coming from all quarters of the globe to get Mr. Meltz to administer his divorces to them.

THE COUPON LETTER OF INTRODUCTION

THE interchange of letters of introduction between old friends, by which valuable acquaintances are added to the list, is a great blessing, and in good hands these letters have, no doubt, been the beginning of many a warm friendship; but, like all other blessings, it has been greatly abused. I have been the recipient of letters, presented by tourists, which, it was easy to see, had been wrung from some sandbagged friend of mine—letters with sobs between the lines, letters punctuated with invisible signals, calling upon me to remember that the bearer had looked over the writer's shoulder as each sentence grew into a polite prevarication.

To those who are in the habit of giving hearty letters of introduction and endorsement to casual acquaintances, I desire to say that I am perfecting a system by which the drugged and kidnapped writer of a style of assumed sincerity and bogus hilarity will be thoroughly protected.

Let me explain briefly and then illustrate my method.

A casual acquaintance, who has met you, say four or five times, and who feels thoroughly intimate with you, calling you by the name that no one uses but your wife, approaches you with an air of confidence that betrays his utter ignorance of himself, and asks for a letter of introduction (in the same serious vein in which one asks for a match). You are already provided with my numbered Introductory Letter Pad. You write the letter of introduction on a sheet numbered to correspond with a letter of advice mailed simultaneously to the person who is to submit to the letter of introduction.

For instance, a young man, inclined to be fresh, enters your office or library and states that he is going abroad. He has learned that you are intimate with Dom Pedro, of Brazil. Perhaps you have conveyed that idea unintentionally while in the young man's presence at some time. So now he asks the trifling favor of a letter of introduction to the Emperor. He is going to see the President and Cabinet and the members of the Supreme Court before he leaves this country, and when he goes to South America he naturally wants to meet Dom Pedro.

So you fill out the right-hand end or coupon of the sheet as follows:

[International Introductory Letter System, Form Z 23.]

No. B 135,986.

New York, Dec. 25,1886.

Sir: You will please honor this letter of introduction in accordance with the terms of a certain letter of advice numbered as above, and bearing even date herewith, mailed to you this day, and oblige, Yours, etc.,

A. B.

The young man goes abroad with this letter inclosed in a maroon alligator-skin pocket-book, and when he arrives in Brazil he finds that the way has been paved for him by the following letter of advice:

[International Introductory Letter System, Form Z 23,] New York, Dec. 25, 1886.

No. B 135,986.

Sir: Mr. W———, a young man with great assurance and a maroon-colored alligator-skin pocket-book, bearing a letter of introduction to you numbered as above, is now at large. He will visit Europe for a few weeks, after which he will tour about South America. He will make a specialty of volcanoes and monarchs.

He will offer to exchange photographs with you, but you must use your own judgment about complying with this request. Do not allow this letter to influence you in the matter.

You will readily recognize him by the wonderful confidence which he has in himself, and which is not shared by those who know him here.

He is a fluent conversationalist, and can talk for hours without fatigue to himself.

You will find it very difficult to wound his feelings, but there would be no harm in trying.

Should you get this letter in time, you might do as you thought best in the matter of quarantine. Some foreign powers are doing that way.

Mr. W———has met a great many prominent people in this country. What this country needs is more free trade on the high seas and better protection for its prominent people.

I have tried to be conservative in what I have said here, and if I have given you a better opinion of the young man than his conduct on fuller acquaintance will warrant, I assure you that I have not done so intentionally.

You will notice at once that he is a self-made man, so your admiration for the works of nature need not be in any way diminished. With due respect, your most obedient servant,

A. B.

To his Imperial Highness D. Pedro, Esq.,

Brazil, S. A.

No. Z 30,805.

Sir: This letter of advice will probably precede a tall youth named Brindley. Mr. Brindley is a young man who, by a strange combination of circumstances, is the eldest son of a perfect gentleman, who now has, and will ever continue to have, my highest esteem and my promissory note for $250.

Will you kindly bear this in mind while you peruse my pleading letter of introduction, which will accompany Mr. Brindley, Jr.?

All through his stormy and tempestuous career in the capacity of son to his father, he has never done anything that the grand jury could get hold of. Treat him as well as you can consistently, and if you can get him a position in a bank, I am sure his father would appreciate it. A place in a bank, where he would not have anything to do but look pretty and declare dividends in a shrill falsetto voice, would please him very much. He is a very good declaimer. He is not accustomed to manual toil, but he has always yearned to do literary work. If he could do the editorial work connected with the sight-draft department, or write humorous indorsements on the backs of checks, over a *nom deplume*, it would tickle the boy almost to death. Anything you could do toward getting him a position in a large bank that is nailed down securely, would be thoroughly appreciated by me, and I should be glad to retaliate at any time.

Yours candidly,

Wyman Dayton.

To Mr. K. O. Peck, London.

A beautiful feature of this invaluable system is the understanding to which everybody is committed, that the original letter is entirely worthless on its presentation unless the letter of advice has been already received.

HOW TO TEACH JOURNALISM

I AM GLAD to know Cornell University is to I establish a department of journalism next September. I have always claimed that journalism could be taught in universities and colleges just as successfully as any other athletic exercise. Of course you cannot teach a boy how to jerk a giant journal from the clutches of decay and make of it a robust and rip snorting shaper and trimmer of public opinion, in whose counting-room people will walk all over each other in their mad efforts to insert advertisements. You cannot teach this in a school any more than you can teach a boy how to discover the open Polar Sea, but you can teach him the rudiments and save him a good deal of time experimenting with himself.

Boys spend small fortunes and the best years of their lives learning the simplest truths in relation to journalism. We grope on blindly, learning this year perhaps how to distinguish an italic shooting-stick when we see it, or how to eradicate type lice from a standing galley, learning next year how to sustain life on an annual pass and a sample early-rose potato weighing four pounds and measuring eleven inches in circumference. This is a slow and tedious way to obtain journalistic training. If this can be avoided or abbreviated it will be a great boon.

As I understand it, the department in Cornell University will not deal so much with actual newspaper experience as it will with construction and style in writing. This is certainly a good move, for we must admit that we can improve very greatly our style and the purity of our English. For instance, I select an exchange at random, and on the telegraphic page I find the details of a horrible crime. It seems that an old lady, who lived by herself almost, and who had amassed between $16 and $17, was awakened by an assassin, dragged from her bed and cruelly murdered. The large telegraph headline reads: "Drug from her bed and murdered!" This is incorrect in orthography, syntax and prosody, bad in form and inelegant in style. Carefully parsing the word drug as it appears here, I find that it does not agree with anything in number, gender or person. I do not like to criticise the style of others when I know that my own is so faulty, but I am sure that the word drug should not be used in this way.

Take the following, also, from the Kansas correspondence of the Statesville (N.C.) *Landmark*:

"There were several bad accidents in and around Clear Water during my absence from home. The saddest one was the shooting of one Peter Peterson by his father. They were out rabbit-hunting in the snow. A rabbit got up and started to run. The son was in a swag of a place and the father was taking aim at the rabbit. The son at the same time was trying to get a shot at it and, not knowing that his father was shooting, ran between the rabbit and his father and was killed dead, falling on the snow with his gun grasped in his hands and never moved. He still carried that pleasant smile which he had on, in expectation of shooting that jack rabbit, when put in the grave. Wheat is selling at about 60 cents; corn, 40 to 50 cents; fat hogs, gross, 44 to 41; fat steers, 41; butcher's stock, 2 cents."

It is hard to say just exactly wherein this is faulty, but something is the matter with it. I would like to get an expression of opinion from those who take an interest in such things, as to whether the fault is in orthoepy, orthography, anatomy, obituary or price current, or whether it consists in writing several features too closely in the same paragraph.

It would also be a good idea to establish a chair for advertisers in some practical college, in order that they might run in for a few hours and learn how to write an advertisement so that it would express in the most direct way what they desired to state. Here is an advertisement, for instance, which is given exactly as written and punctuated:

Mrs. Dr. Edwards,

THE GREAT WESTERN CLAIRVOYANT,

Has arrived, and-will remain only a short time. Call at once at HOTEL WINDSOR, 119, 121 and 123 East State street, Room 19, third floor. Please take elevator.

The greatest and most natural born, and highly celebrated, and well-known all over the country, Clairvoyant, now traveling on the road, and Wonder from the Pacific coast.

Seventh Daughter of the Seventh Daughter; born with veil and second sight; every mystery revealed; if one you love is true or false; removes trouble; settles lovers' quarrels; causes a speedy marriage with one you Jove; valuable information to gentlemen on all business transactions; how to make profitable investments for speedy riches; lucky numbers; Egyptian talisman for the un lucky; cures mysterious and chronic diseases. All who are sick or in trouble from any cause are invited to call without delay.

I have always claimed that clairvoyance could be made a success if we could find some one who was sufficiently natural born to grapple with it. Now, Mrs. Edwards seems to know what is required. She was born utterly without affectation. When she was born she just seemed to say to those who happened to be present at the time, "Fellow citizens, you will have to take me just as you find me. I cannot dissemble or appear to be otherwise than what I am. I am the most natural born and highly celebrated all over the country clairvoyant now traveling on the road, and Wonder from the Pacific coast." She then let off a whoop that ripped open the sable robes of night, after which she took a light lunch and retired to her dressing-room.

Ex-Mayor Henry C. Robinson, of Hartford, Conn., if I am not mistaken, suggested a school of journalism at least twelve years ago, but it did not meet with immediate and practical indorsement. Now Cornell comes forward and seems to be in earnest, and I am glad of it. The letters received from day to day by editors, and written to them by men engaged in other pursuits, practically admit and prove that there is not now in existence an editor who knows enough to carry liver to a bear.

That is the reason why every means should be used to pull this profession out of the mire of dense ignorance and place it upon the high, dry soil which leads to genius and consanguinity.

The above paragraph I quote from a treatise on journalism which I wrote just before I knew anything about it.

The life of the journalist is a hard one, and, although it is not so trying as the life of the newspaper man, it is full of trials and perplexities. If newspaper men and journalists did not stand by each other I do not know what joy they would have. Kindness for each other, gentleness and generosity, even in their rivalry, characterize the conduct of a large number of them.

I shall never forget my first opportunity to do a kind act for a fellow newspaper man, nor with what pleasure I availed myself of it, though he was my rival, especially in the publication of large and spirited equestrian handbills and posters. He also printed a rival paper and assailed me most bitterly from time to time. His name was Lorenzo Dow Pease, and we had carried on an acrimonious warfare for two years. He had said that I was a reformed Prohibitionist and that I had left a neglected wife in every State in the Union. I had stated that he would give better satisfaction if he would wear his brains breaded. Then he had said something else that was personal and it had gone on so for some time. We devoted fifteen minutes each day to the management of our respective papers, and the balance of the day to doing each other up in a way to please our subscribers.

One evening Lorenzo Dow Pease came into my office and said he wanted to see me personally. I said that would suit me exactly and that if he had asked to see me in any other way I did not know how I could have arranged it. He said he meant that he would like to see me by myself. I therefore discharged the force, turned out the dog and we had the office to ourselves. I could see that he was in trouble, for every little while he would brush away a tear in an underhanded kind of way and swallow a large, imaginary mass of something. I asked Lorenzo why he felt so depressed, and he said: "William, I have came here for a favor." He always said "I have came," for he was a self-made man and hadn't done a very good job either. "I have came here for a favor. I wrote a reply to your venomous attack of to-day and I expected to publish it to-morrow in my paper, but, to tell you the truth, we are out of paper. At least, we have a few bundles at the freight office, but they have taken to sending it C. O. D., and I haven't the means just at hand to take it out. Now, as a brother in the great and glorious order of journalism, would it be too much for you to loan me a couple of bundles of paper to do me till I get my pay for some equestrian bills struck off Friday and just as good as the wheat?"

"How long would a couple of bundles last you?" I asked as I looked out at the window and wondered if he would reveal his circulation.

"Five issues and a little over," he said, filling his pipe from a small box on the desk.

"But you could cut off your exchanges and then it would last longer," I remarked.

"Yes, but only for one additional issue. I am very anxious to appear to-morrow, because my subscribers will be looking for a reply to what you said about me this morning. You stated that I was 'a journalistic bacteria looking for something to infect,' and while I did not come here to get you to retract, I would like it as a favor if you would loan me enough white paper to set myself straight before my subscribers."

"Well, why don't you go and tell them about it? It wouldn't take long," I said in a jocund way, slapping Lorenzo on the back. But he did not laugh. I then told him that we only had paper enough to last us till our next bill came, and so I could not possibly loan any, but that if he would write a caustic reply to my editorial I would print it for him. He caught me in his arms and then for a moment his head was pillowed on my breast. Then he sat down and wrote the following card:

Editor of the Boomerang:

Will you allow me through your columns to state that in your issue of yesterday you did me a great injustice by referring to me as a journalistic bacteria looking for something to infect; also, as a lop eared germ of contagion, and warning people to vaccinate in order to prevent my spread? I denounce the whole article as a malicious falsehood, and state that if you will only give me a chance I will fight you on sight. All I ask is that you will wait till I can overtake you, and I am able and willing to knock great chunks off the universe with you. I do not ask any favors of an editor who misleads his subscribers and intentionally misunderstands his correspondents; a man who advises an anxious inquirer who wants to know "how to get a cheap baby buggy" to leave the child at a cheap hotel; a man who assumes to wear brains, but who really thinks with a fungus growth; a man the bleak and barren exterior of whose head is only equalled by its bald and echoing interior.

Lorenzo Dow Pease.

I looked it over, and as there didn't seem to be anything personal in it, I told him I would print it for him with pleasure. He then asked that I would, as a further favor, refrain from putting any advertising marks on it and that I would make it follow pure reading matter, which I did. I leaded the card and printed it with a simple word of introduction, in which I said that I took pleasure in printing it, inasmuch as Mr. Pease could not get his paper out of the express office for a few days. It was a kindness to him and did not hurt my paper in the end.

There are many reasons why the establishment of a department of journalism at Cornell will be a good move, and I believe that while it will not take the place of actual experience, it will serve to shorten the apprenticeship of a young newspaper man and the fatigue of starting the amateur in journalism will be divided between the managing editor and the tutor. It will also give the aspiring sons of wealthy parents a chance to toy with journalism without interfering with those who are actually engaged in it.

HIS GARDEN

I ALWAYS enjoy a vegetable garden, and through the winter I look forward to the spring days when I will take my cob pipe and hoe and go joyously afield. I like to toy with the moist earth and the common squash bug of the work-a-day world. It is a pleasure also to irrigate the garden, watering the sauer kraut plant and the timid tomato vine as though they were children asking for a drink. I am never happier than when I am engaged in irrigating my tropical garden or climbing my neighbor with a hoe when he shuts off my water supply by sticking an old pair of pantaloons in the canal that leads to my squash conservatory.

One day a man shut off my irrigation that way and dammed the water up to such a degree that I shut off his air supply, and I was about to say dammed him up also. We had quite a scuffle. Up to that time we had never exchanged a harsh word. That morning I noticed that my early climbing horse-radish and my dwarf army worms were looking a little au revoir, and I wondered what was the matter. I had been absent several days and was grieved to notice that my garden had a kind of blase air, as though it needed rest and change of scene.

The Poland China egg-plant looked up sadly at me and seemed to say: "Pardner, don't you think it's a long time between drinks?" The watermelon seemed to have a dark brown taste in its mouth, and there was an air of gloom all over the garden.

At that moment I discovered my next-door neighbor at the ditch on the corner. He was singing softly to himself:

O, yes, I'll meet you;

I'll meet you when the sun goes down.

He was also jamming an old pair of Rembrandt pants into the canal, where they would shut off my supply. He stood with his back towards me, and just as he said he would "meet me when the sun went down," I smote him across the back of the neck with my hoe handle, and before he could recover from the first dumb surprise and wonder, I pulled the dripping pantaloons out of the ditch and tied them in a true-lover's knot around his neck. He began to look black in the face, and his struggles soon ceased altogether. At that moment his wife came out and shrieked two pure womanly shrieks, and hissed in my ear: "You have killed me husband!"

I said, possibly I had. If so, would she please send in the bill and I would adjust it at an early day. I said this in a bantering tone of voice, and raising my hat to her in that polished way of mine, started to go, when something fell with a thud on the greensward!

It was the author of these lines. I did not know till two days afterward that my neighbor's wife wore a moire antique rolling-pin under her apron that morning. I did not suspect it till it was too late. The affair was kind of hushed up on account of the respectability of the parties.

By the time I had recovered the garden seemed to melt away into thin air. My neighbor had it all his own way, and while his proud hollyhocks and Johnny-jump-ups reared their heads to drink the mountain water at the twilight hour, my little, low-necked, summer squashes curled up and died.

Most every year yet I made a garden. I pay a man $3 to plow it. Then I pay $7.50 for garden seeds and in July I hire the same man at $3 to summer-fallow the whole thing while I go and buy my vegetables of a Chinaman named Wun Lung. I've done this now for eight years, and I owe my robust health and rich olive complexion to the fact that I've got a garden and do just as little in it as possible. Parties desiring a dozen or more of my Shanghai egg-plants to set under an ordinary domestic hen can procure the same by writing to me and enclosing lock of hair and $10.

WRITTEN TO THE BOY

Asheville, N. C., Feb. 10,1887.

MY DEAR HENRY: Your last issue of the *Retina*, your new thought vehicle, published at New Belony, this state, was received yesterday. I like this number, I think, better than I did the first. While the news in it seems fresher, the editorial assertions are not so fresh. You do not state that you "have come to stay" this week, but I infer that you occupy the same position you did last week with inference to that.

I was more especially interested in your piece about how to rear children and the care of parents. I read it to your mother last night while she was setting her bread. Nothing tickles me very often at my time of life, and when I laugh a loud peal of laughter at anything nowadays it's got to be a pretty blamed good thing, I can tell you that. But your piece about bringing up children made me laugh real hard. I enjoy a piece like that from the pen of a juicy young brain like yours. It almost made me young again to read the words of my journalistic gosling son.

You also say that "teething is the most trying time for parents." Do you mean that parents are more fretful when they are teething than any other time? Your mother and me reckoned that you must mean that. If so, it shows your great research. How a mere child hardly out of knee-panties, a young shoot like you, who was never a parent for a moment in his life, can enter into and understand the woes that beset parents is more than I can understand. If you had been through what I have while teething I could see how you might understand and write about it, but at present I do not see through it. The first teeth I cut as a parent made me very restless. I was sick two years ago with a new disease that was just out and the doctor gave me something for it that made my teeth fall like the leaves of autumn. In six weeks after I began to convalesce my mouth was perfectly bald-headed. For days I didn't bite into a Ben Davis apple that I didn't leave a fang into it.

Well, after that I saw an advertisement in the *Rural Rustler*—a paper I used to take then—of a place where you could get a set of teeth for $6.

I didn't want to buy a high-priced and gaudy set of teeth at the tail end of such a life as I had led, and I knew that teeth, no matter how expensive they might be, would be of little avail to coming generations, so I went over to the place named in the paper and got an impression of my mouth taken.

There is really nothing in this life that will take the stiff-necked pride out of a man like viewing a plaster cast of his tottering mouth. The dentist fed me with a large ladle full of putty or plaster of paris, I reckon, and told me to hold it in my mouth till it set.

I don't remember a time in all my life when the earth and transitory things ever looked so undesirable and so trifling as they did while I sat there in that big red barber-chair with my mouth full of cold putty. I felt just as a man might when he is being taxidermied.

After awhile the dentist took out the cast. It was a cloudy day and so it didn't look much like me after all. If it had I would have sent you one. After I'd set again two or three times, we got a pretty fair likeness, he said, and I went home, having paid $6 and left my address.

Three weeks after that a small boy came with my new teeth.

They were nice, white, shiny teeth, and did not look very ghastly after I had become used to them. I wished at first that the gums had been a duller red and that the teeth had not looked so new. I put them in my mouth, but they felt cold and distant. I took them out and warmed them in the sunlight. People going by no doubt thought that I did it to show that I was able to have new teeth, but that was not the case.

I wore them all that forenoon while I butchered. There were times during the forenoon when I wanted to take them out, but when a man is butchering he hates to take his teeth out just because they hurt.

Neighbors told me that after my mouth got hardened on the inside it would feel better.

But, oh, how it relieved me at night to take those teeth out and put them on the top of a cool bureau, where the wind could blow through their whiskers! How I hated to resume them in the morning and start in on another long day, when the roof of my mouth felt like a big, red bunion and my gums like a pale red stone-bruise.

A year ago, Henry, about two-thirty in the afternoon I think it was, I left that set of teeth in the rare flank of a barbecue I was to in our town.

Since then I have not been so pretty, perhaps, but I have no more unicorns on the rafters of my mouth and my note is just as good at thirty days as ever it was.

You are right, Henry, when you go on to state in your paper that teething is the most trying time for parents.

Ta, ta, as the feller says.

Your father.

ANSWERS TO CORRESPONDENTS

George E. Beath, Areola, Ill.,-writes to know "the value of a silver dollar of 1878 with eight feathers in the eagle's tail."

It is worth what you can get for it, Mr. Beath. Perhaps the better way would be to forward it to me and I will do the best I can with it. There being but eight feathers in the eagle's tail would be no drawback. Send it to me at once and I will work it off for you, Mr. Beath.

"Tutor," Tucson, Ariz., asks "What do you regard as the best method of teaching the alphabet to children?"

Very likely my method would hardly receive your indorsement, but with my own children I succeed by using an alphabet with the names attached, which I give below. I find that by connecting the alphabet with certain easy and interesting subjects the child rapidly acquires knowledge of the letter, and it becomes firmly fixed in the mind. I use the following list of alphabetical names in the order given below:

A is for Antediluvian, Anarchistic and Agamemnon.

B is for Bucephalus, Burgundy and Bull-head. C is for Cantharides, Confucius and Casabianca. D is for Deuteronomy, Delphi and Dishabille.

E is for Euripedes, European and Effervescent. F is for Fumigate, Farinaceous and Fundamental.

G is for Garrulous, Gastric and Gangrene.

H is for Hamestrap, Honeysuckle and Hoyle.

I is for Idiosyncrasy, Idiomatic and Iodine.

J is for Jaundice, Jamaica and Jeu-d'esprit.

K is for Kandilphi, Kindergarten and KuKlux. L is for Lop-sided, Lazarus and Llano Estacado. M is for Menengitis, Mardi Gras and Mesopotamia.

N is for Narragansett, Neapolitan and Nix-comarous.

Q is for Oleander, Oleaginous and Oleomargarine.

P is for Phlebotomy, Phthisic and Parabola.

Q is for Query, Quasi and Quits.

R is for Rejuvenate, Regina and Requiescat.

S is for Simultaneous, Sigauche and Saleratus.

T is for Tubercular, Themistocles and Thereabouts.

U is for Ultramarine, Uninitiated and Utopian.

V is for Voluminous, Voltaire and Vivisection. W is for Witherspoon, Woodcraft and Washerwoman.

X is for Xenophon, Xerxes and Xmas.

Y is for Ysdle, Yahoo and Yellowjacket.

Z is for Zoological, Zanzibar and Zacatecas.

In this way the eye of the child is first appealed to. He becomes familiar with the words which begin with a certain letter, and before he knows it the letter itself has impressed itself upon his memory.

Sometimes, however, where my children were slow to remember a word and hence its corresponding letter, I have drawn the object on a blackboard or on the side of the barn. For instance, we will suppose that D is hard to fix in the mind of the pupil and the words to which it belongs as an initial do not readily cling to memory. I have only to draw upon the board a Deuteronomy, a Delphi, or a Dishabille, and he will never forget it. No matter how he may struggle to do so, it will still continue to haunt his brain forever. The same with Z, which is a very difficult letter to remember. I assist the memory by stimulating the eye, drawing rapidly, and crudely perhaps, a Zoological, a Zanzibar or a Zacatecas.

The great difficulty in teaching children the letters is that there is really nothing in the naked alphabet itself to win a child's love. We must dress it in attractive colors and gaudy plumage so that he will be involuntarily drawn to it.

Those who have used my method say that after mastering the alphabet, the binomial theorum and the rule in Shelly's case seemed like child's play. This goes to show what method and discipline will accomplish in the mind of the young.

"Fond Mother," Braley's Fork, asks: "What shall I name my little girl baby?"

That will depend upon yourself very largely, "Fond Mother." Very likely if your little girl is very rugged and grows up to be the fat woman in a museum, she will wear the name of Lily. When a girl is named Lily, she at once manifests a strong desire to grow up with a complexion like Othello and the same fatal yearning for some one to strangle. This is not always thus, but girls are obstinate, and it is better not to put a name on a girl baby that she will not live up to.

Again, "Fond Mother," let me urge you to refrain from naming your little daughter a soft, flabby name like Irma, Geraldine, Bandoline, Lilelia, Potassa, Valerian, Rosetta or Castoria. These names belong to the inflammatory pages of the American novelette. Do not put such a name on your innocent child. Imagine this inscription on a marble slab:

TRIFOLIATA,

BELOVED DAUGHTER OF

GERALD AND VASELINE TUBBS,

DIED MARCH 27,1888.

SHE CAUGHT COLD IN HER FRONT NAME

I have seen a young lady try faithfully for years to live down one of these flimsy, cheesecloth names, but the harsh world would not have it. A good name is rather to be chosen than great riches, and while I can imagine your little girl in future years as a white-haired and lovely grandmother, wearing the name of Mary or Ruth, with a double chin that seems to ever beckon the old gentleman to come and chuck his fat forefinger under it, I cannot, in my mind's eye, see her as a household deity, wearing a white cap and the name of Rosette or Penumbra, or Sogodontia, or Catalpa, or Voxliumania.

THE FARMER AND THE TARIFF

ON BOARD a western train the other day I held in my bosom for over seventy-five miles the elbow of a large man whose name I do not know. He was not a railroad hog or I would have resented it. He was built wide and he couldn't help it, so I forgave him.

He had a large, gentle, kindly eye, and when he desired to spit he went to the car door, opened it and decorated the entire outside of the train, forgetting that our speed would help to give scope to his remarks.

Naturally, as he sat there by my side, holding on tightly to his ticket and evidently afraid the conductor would forget to come and get it, I began to figure out in my mind what might be his business. He had pounded one thumb so that the nail was black where the blood had settled under it. This might happen to a shoemaker, a carpenter, a blacksmith, or almost any one else. So it didn't help me out much, though it looked to me as though it might have been done by trying to drive a fence-nail through a leather hinge with the back of an ax, and nobody but a farmer would try to do that. Following up the clew, I discovered that he had milk on his boots, and then I knew I was right. The man who milks before daylight in a dark barn when the thermometer is 28° below zero, and who hits his boots by reason of the uncertain light and prudishness of the cow, is a marked man. He cannot conceal the fact that he is a farmer unless he removes that badge. So I started out on that theory, and remarked that this would pass for a pretty hard winter on stock. The thought was not original with me, for I have heard it expressed by others either in this country or Europe. He said it would.

"My cattle has gone through a mowful o' hay since October and eleven ton o' brand. Hay don't seem to have the goodness to it thet it hed last year, and with their new process griss mills they jerk all the juice out o' brand, so's you might as well feed cows with excelsior and upholster your horses with hemlock bark as to buy brand."

"Well, why do you run so much to stock? Why don't you try diversified farming and rotation of crops?"

"Well, prob'ly you got that idee in the papers. A man that earns big wages writing 'Farm Hints' for agricultural papers can make more money with a soft lead-pencil and two or three season-cracked idees like that 'n I can carrying of 'em out on the farm. We used to have a feller in the drug-store in our town that wrote such good pieces for the *Rural Vermonter*, and made up such a good condition powder out of his own head that two years ago we asked him to write a nessay for the annual meeting of the Buckwheat Trust, and to use his own judgment about choice of subject. And what do you s'pose he had selected for a nessey that took the whole forenoon to read?"

"What subject, you mean?"

"Yes."

"Give it up!"

"Well, he'd wrote out that whole blamed intellectual wad on the subject of 'The Inhumanity of Dehorning Hydraulic Rams.' How's that?"

"That's pretty fair."

"Well, farmin' is like runnin' a paper in regard to some things. Every feller in the world will take and turn in and tell you how to do it, even if he don't know a blame thing about it. There ain't a man in the United States to-day that don't secretly think he could run airy one if his other business busted on him, whether he knows the difference between a new milch cow or a horse hayrake or not. We had one of these embroidered nightshirt farmers come from town better'n three years ago. Been a toilet-soap man and done well, and so he came out and bought a farm that had nothing to it but a fancy house and barn, a lot of medder in the front yard, and a Southern aspect. The farm was no good. You couldn't raise a disturbance on it. Well, what does he do? Goes and gits a passle of slim-tailed yeller cows from New Jersey and aims to handle cream and diversified farming. Last year the cuss sent a load of cream over and tried to sell it at the new crematory while the funeral and hollercost was goin' on. I may be a sort of a chump myself, but I read my paper and don't get left like that."

"What are the prospects for farmers in your State?"

"Well, they are pore. Never was so pore, in fact, sence I've ben there. Folks wonder why boys leaves the farm. My boys left so as to get protected, they said, and so they went into a clothing store, one of 'em, and one went into hardware, and one is talkin' protection in the Legislature this winter. They said that farmin' was gettin' to be like fishin' and huntin', well enough for a man that has means and leisure, but they couldn't make a livin' at it, they said. Another boy is in a drug store, and the man that hires him says he is a royal feller."

"Kind of a castor royal feller," I said, with a shriek of laughter.

He waited until I had laughed all I wanted to, and then he said:

"I've always hollered for high tariff in order to hyst the public debt, but now that we've got the National debt coopered I wish they'd take a little hack at mine. I've put in fifty years farmin'. I never drank licker in any form. I've worked from ten to eighteen hours a day; been economical in cloz and never went to a show more'n a dozen times in my life; raised a family and learned upwards of two hundred calves to drink out of a tin pail without blowing their vittles up my sleeve. My wife worked alongside o' me sewin' new seats on the boys' pants, skim-min' milk, and even helpin' me load hay. For forty years we toiled along together and hardly got time to look into each other's faces or dared to stop and get acquainted with each other. Then her health failed. Ketched cold in the springhouse, prob'ly skimmin' milk, and wash-in' pans, and scaldin' pails, and spankin' butter. Anyhow, she took in a long breath one day while the doctor and me was watchin' her, and she says to me, 'Henry,' says she, 'I've got a chance to rest,' and she put one tired, wore-out hand on top of the other tired, wore-out hand, and I knew she'd gone where they don't work all day and do chores all night.

"I took time to kiss her then. I'd been too busy for a good while previous to do that, and then I called in the boys. After the funeral it was too much for them to stay around and eat the kind of cookin' we had to put up with, and nobody spoke up around the house as we used to. The boys quit whistlin' around the barn, and talked kind of low to themselves about goin' to town and getting a job.

"They're all gone now, and the snow is four feet deep up there on mother's grave in the old berryin'-ground."

Then both of us looked out of the car-window quite a long while without saying anything.

"I don't blame the boys for going into something else long's other things pays better; but I say—and I say what I know—that the man who holds the prosperity of this country in his hands, the man that actually makes the money for other people to spend, the man that eats three good, simple, square meals a day and goes to bed at 9 o'clock so that future generations with good blood and cool brains can go from his farm to the Senate and Congress and the White House—he is the man that gets left at last to run his farm, with nobody to help him but a hired man and a high protective tariff. The farms in our State is mortgaged for over $700,000,000. Ten of our Western States—I see by the papers—has got about three billion and a half mortgages on their farms, and that don't count the chattel mortgages filed with the town clerks on farm machinery, stock, waggins, and even crops, by gosh! that ain't two inches high under the snow. That's what the prospect is for farms now. The Government is rich, but the men that made it, the men that fought perarie fires and perarie wolves and Injins and potato bugs and blizzards, and has paid the war debt and pensions and everything else, and hollored for the Union and the Republican party and high tariff and anything else that they was told to, is left high and dry this cold winter with a mortgage of seven billions and a half on the farms they have earned and saved a thousand times over."

"Yes; but look at the glory of sending from the farm the future President, the future Senator and the future member of Congress."

"That looks well on paper; but what does it really amount to? Soon as a farmer boy gits in a place like that he forgets the soil that produced and holds his head as high as a hollyhock. He bellers for protection to everybody but the farmer, and while he sails round in a highty-tighty room with a fire in it night and day, his father on the farm has to kindle his own fire in the morning with elm slivers, and he has to wear his son's lawn-tennis suit next to him or freeze to death, and he has to milk in an old gray shawl that has held that member of Congress since he was a baby, by gorry! and the old lady has to sojourn through the winter in the flannels that Silas wor at the rigatter before he went to Congress.

"So I say, and I think that Congress agrees with me, Damn a farmer, anyhow!"

He then went away.

A CONVENTIONAL SPEECH

DURING the recent conventions a great many good speeches have been made which did not get into print for various reasons. Some others did not even get a hearing and still others were prepared by delegates who could not get the eye of the presiding officer.

The manuscript of the following speech bears the marks of earnest thought, and though the author did not obtain recognition on the floor of the convention I cannot bear to see an appreciative public deprived of it:

MR. Chairman and Gentlemen of the Convention: We are met together here as a representation of the greatest and grandest party in the world—a party that has been first in peace, first in war and first in the hearts of its countrymen, as the good book has it. We come together here to-day, Gentlemen, to perpetuate by our action the principles which won us victory at the polls and wrenched it from an irritated and disagreeable foe on many a tented field. I refer to freedom.

Our party has ever been the champion of freedom. We have made a specialty of freedom. We have ever been in the van. That's why we have been on the move. Where freedom a quarter of a century ago was but a mere name, now we have fostered it and aided it and encouraged it and made it pay.

We have emancipated a whole race, several of whom have since voted the other way. But we must not be discouraged. We are here to work. Let us do it and so advance our common cause and honor God.

But who is to be the leader? Who will be able to carry our victorious banner from Portland, Me., to Portland, Ore., gayly speaking pieces from the tail-gate of a train? Who is sufficiently obscure to safely make the race? (Cries of "Jeremiah M. Rusk," "Rudolph Minkins Pitler," "Blaine," "James Swartout," "John Sherman," "Charlie Kinney," &c.)

The eye of the nation is upon us. We cannot escape the awful responsibility which we have to-day assumed. With all our anxiety to please our friends we must not forget that we are here in the interests of universal freedom. Do not allow yourselves to be blinded, gentlemen, by the assurance that this is to be a businessman's campaign, a campaign in which conflicting business interests are to figure more than the late war. It is a fight involving universal freedom, as I said in our conventions four, eight and twelve years ago.

We have before us a pure and highly elocutionary platform. Let us nominate a man who will, as I may say, affilliate and amalgamate with that platform. Who is that man? (Cries of "Blaine, Blaine, James G. Blaine," "Lockwood, Lockwood, Belva A. Lockwood," and general confusion, during which John A. Wise is seen to jerk loose about a nickel's worth of Billy Mahone's whiskers.)

Mr. Chairman and Gentlemen of the convention, there has never been a more harmonious convention in the United States to my knowledge since the Sioux massacre in Minnesota. We are all here for the best good of the party and each is willing to concede something rather than create any ill-feeling. Look at Mahone for instance.

We have a good platform, now let us nominate a man whose record is in harmony with that platform. Freedom has ever been our watchword. Now that we have made the human race within our borders absolutely free, let us add to our magnificent history as a party by one crowning act. Let us fight for the Emancipation of Rum!

Rum has always been a mighty power in American politics, but it has not been absolutely free. Let us be the first to recognize it as the great corner-stone of American institutions. Let us make it free.

We have never had any Daniel Websters or Henry Clays since rum went up from 20 cents a gallon to its present price. The war tax on whiskey for over twenty years has made freedom a farce and liberty a loud and empty snort in mid-air. 'Who, then, shall be our standard-bearer as we journey onward towards victory? (Cries of "Blaine, Blaine, James G. Blaine," and confusion.)

Gentlemen, I wish that a better and thrillinger orator had been selected in my place to name the candidate on whom alone I can unite. Soldiers, rail-splitters, statesmen, canal boys, tailors, farmers, merchants and school teachers have been Presidents of the United States, but to my knowledge no convention has ever yet named a distiller. I have the honor to-day to name a modest man for the high office of President; a man who never before allowed his name to be presented to a convention; a man who never even stated in the papers that his name would not be presented to the convention; a man who has never sought or courted publicity even in his own business; a man who has been a distiller in a quiet way for over fifteen years and yet has never even advertised in the papers; a man who has so carefully shunned the eye of the world that only two or three of us know where his place of business is; a man who has such an utter contempt for office that he has shot two Government officials who claimed to be connected with the internal revenue business; a man who can drink or let it alone, but who has aimed to divide the time up about equally between the two; a man who had absolutely nothing to do with the war, not having heard about it in time; a man who defies his culumniators or anybody else of his heft; a man who would paint the White House red; a man who takes great pleasure in being his own worst enemy. (Cries of "Name him! Name him!" Great confusion, and cries of pain from several harmonious delegates who are getting the worst of it.)

Not to take up your time, let me say in closing that the day for great men as candidates for an important office is past. Great men in a great country antagonize different factions and are then compelled to fall back on literature. What we want is an obscure and silent chump. I have found him. He has never antagonized but two men in his life and they are now voting in a better land. He is a plain man, and his career at Washington would be marked with more or less tobacco juice. For over fifteen years he has been constructing at his country seat a lurid style of whiskey known as The Essence of Crime. Quietly and unostentatiously he has fought for the emancipation of whiskey everywhere. He says that we are too prone to worry about our clothes and their cost and to give too little thought to our tax-ridden rum.

Then, Mr. Chairman and Gentlemen, here in the full glare of public approval, feeling that the name I am about to pronounce will in a few moments flash across a mighty continent and greet the moist and moaning news editor, the grimy peasant, the pussy banker and the streaked tennis player; that the name I now nourish in my panting brain will soon be taken up on willing tongues and borne across the union, rising and saluting the hot blue dome of heaven, pulsating across the ocean, rocking the beautifully upholstered thrones of the Old World and calling forth a dark blue torrent of profanity from the offices of the illustrated papers, none of which will be provided with his portrait, I desire to name Mr. Clem Beasly, of Arkansaw, a man who has spent his best years manufacturing man's greatest enemy. I hurrah for him and holler for him, and love him for the (hic) enemy he has made.

A PLEA FOR ONE IN ADVERSITY

I LEARN with much sadness that Mr. William H. Vanderbilt's once princely fortune has shrivelled down to $150,000,000. This piece of information comes to me like a clap of thunder out of a clear sky. Once petted, fondled and caressed, William H. Vanderbilt shorn of his wealth, and resting upon no foundation but his sterling integrity, must struggle along with the rest of us.

It would be but truth to say that Mr. Vanderbilt will receive very little sympathy from the world now in the days of his adversity and penury when the wolf is at his door. There are many of his former friends who will say that William could economize and struggle along on $150,000,000, but let them try it once and see how they would like it themselves; $150,000,000, with no salary outside of that amount, will not last forever.

A poor man might pinch along in such a case if he could get something to do, but we must remember that Mr. Vanderbilt has always lived in comparatively comfortable circumstances. His hands, therefore, are tender and his stomach juts out into the autumn air. He will, therefore, find it hard at first to husk corn and dig potatoes. When he stoops over a sawbuck around New York this winter his stomach will be in the way and his vest will no doubt split open on the back. All these things will annoy the spoiled child of luxury, and his broad features will be covered with sadness. They will, at least, if there is sadness enough in the country to do it.

The fall of William 'H. Vanderbilt and his headlong plunge from the proud eminence to which his means had elevated him downward to the cringing poverty of $150,000,000 should be a sad warning to us all. This fate may fall to any of us. Oh, let us be prepared when the summons comes. For one I believe I am ready. Should the dread news come to me to-morrow that such a fate had befallen me, I would nerve myself up to it and meet it like a man. With the ruin of my former fortune I would buy me a crust of bread and some pie, and then I would take the balance and go over into Canada and there I would establish a home for friendless bank cashiers who are now there, several hundred of them, all alone and with no one to love them.

All kinds of charitable institutions, costing many thousands of dollars, are built in America from year to year for the comfort of homeless and friendless women and children, but man is left out in the cold. Why is this thus. Lots of people in Canada, of course, are doing their best to make it cheerful and sunny for our lovely cashiers there, but still it is not home. As a gentleman once said in my hearing, "There is no place like home." And he was right.

In conclusion, I do not know what to say, unless it be to appeal to the newspaper men of the country in Mr. Vanderbilt's behalf. While he was wealthy he was proud and arrogant. He said, "Let the newspapers be blankety blanked to blank," or words to that effect, but we do not care for that. Let us forget all that and remember that his sad fate may some day be our own. In our affluence let us not lose sight of the fact that Van is suffering. Let us procure a place for him on some good paper. His grammar and spelling are a little bit rickety but he could begin as janitor and gradually work his way up. Parties having clothing or funds which they feel like giving may forward the same to me at Hudson, Wis., postpaid, and if the clothes do not fit Van they may possibly fit me.

New York, Oct. 7, 1883.

Bill Nye.

P.S,—Oct. 30.—Since issuing the above I have received several consignments of clothes for the suffering, also one sack of corn-meal and a ham. Let the good work go on, for it is far more blessed to give than to receive, I am told; and as Jay Gould said when, as a boy, he gave the wormy half of an apple to his dear teacher, "Half is better than the hole."

THE RHUBARB-PIE

IN June the medicated tropical fruit known as the rhubarb-pie is in full bloom. The farmer goes forth into his garden to find out where the coy, old setting hen is hiding from the vulgar gaze, and he discovers that his pie-plant is ripe. He then forms a syndicate with his wife for the purpose of publishing the seditious and rebellious pie.

It is singular that the War Department has never looked into the scheme for fighting the Indians with rhubarb-pie, instead of the regular army. One-half the army could then put in its time court-martialing the other half, and all would be well.

Rhubarb undoubtedly has its place in the *materia medica*, but when it sneaks into the pie of commerce it is out of place. Castor-oil, and capsicum, and dynamite, and chloroform, and porous-plasters, and arsenic, all have their uses in one way or another, but they would not presume to enter into the composition of a pie.

They know it would not be tolerated. But rhubarb, elated with its success as a drug, forgets its humble origin and aspires to become au article of diet.

Now the pumpkin knows its place. You never knew of a pumpkin trying to monkey with science. The pumpkin knows that it was born to bury itself in the bosom of the pumpkin-pie. It does not therefore, go about the country claiming to be a remedy for spavin.

Supposing that the gory, yet toothsome steak, that grows on the back of the twenty-one-year-old steer's neck, should claim for itself that it could go into a drug-store and cure rheumatism and heartburn. Wouldn't every one say that it was out of place and uncalled for? Certainly. The back of the tough old steer's neck knows that it is destined for the mince-pie, and nature did not intend otherwise. So also with the vulcanized gristle, and arctic overshoe heel, and the shoe-string, and the white button, and all those elements that go to make up the mince-pie. They do not try to make medicines and cordials and anodynes of themselves. Rhubarb is the only thing that successfully holds its place with the apothecary, and yet draws a salary in the pie business.

I do not know how others may look at this matter, but I do not think it is right. Still you find this medicated pie in the social circle everywhere. We guard our homes with the strictest surveillance in other matters, and yet we allow the low, vulgar pie-plant-pie to creep into our houses and into our hearts. That is, it creeps into our hearts figuratively speaking. The heart is not, as a matter of fact, one of the digestive organs, but I use the term just as all poets do under like circumstances.

Many, however, will always continue to use the rhubarb-pie, and for those I give below a receipt which has stood the test of years,—one which results in a pie that frosts and sudden atmospheric changes cannot injure.

None but the youngest rhubarb should be used in making pies. Go out and kill your rhubarb with a club, taking care not to kill the old and tough variety. Give it a chance to repent. Remove the skin carefully, and take out the digestive economy of the plant. Be specially careful to get off the "fuzzy" coating, as rhubarb-pies with hair on are not in such favor as they were when the country was new. Now put in the basement of cement and throw on your rhubarb. Flavor with linseed-oil, and hammer out the top crust until it is moderately thin. Then solder on the cover and drill holes for the copper rivets. Having headed the rivets in place, nail on zinc monogram, and kiln-dry the pie slowly. When it is cooled, put on two coats of metallic paint, and adjust the time-lock. After you find that the pie is impervious to the action of chilled steel or acids, remove and feed it to the man who cheerfully pays for his whiskey and steals his newspaper.

A COUNTRY FIRE

LAST night I was awakened by the cry of fire. It was a loud, hoarse cry, such as a large, adult man might emit from his window on the night air. The town was not large, and the fire-department, I had been told, was not so effective as it should have been.

For that reason I arose and carefully dressed myself in order to assist, if possible. I carefully lowered myself from my room by means of a staircase which I found concealed in a dark and mysterious corner of the passage.

On the streets all was confusion. The hoarse cry of fire had been taken up by others, passed around from one to another, till it had swollen into a dull roar. The cry of fire in a small town is always a grand sight.

All along the street in front of Mr. Pendergast's roller rink the blanched faces of the people could be seen. Men were hurrying to and fro, knocking the by-standers over in their frantic attempts to get somewhere else. With great foresight Mr. Pendergast, who had that day finished painting his roller rink a dull-roan color, removed from the building the large card which bore the legend

FRESH PAINT!

so that those who were so disposed might feel perfectly free to lean up against the rink and watch the progress of the flames.

Anon the bright glare of the devouring element might have been seen bursting through the casement of Mr. Cicero Williams' residence, facing on the alley west of Mr. Pendergast's rink. Across the street the spectator whose early education had not been neglected could distinctly read the sign of our esteemed fellow-townsman, Mr. Alonzo Burlingame, which was lit up by the red glare of the flames so that the letters stood out plain as follows:

ALONZO BURLINGAME,

Dealer in Soft and Hard Coal, Ice-Cream, Wood, Lime.

Cement, Perfumery, Nails, Putty, Spectacles, and Horse

Radish.

Chocolate Caramels and Tar Roofing.

Gas-Pitting and Undertaking in All Its Branches.

Hides, Tallow and Maple Syrup.

Fine Gold Jewelry, Silverware and Salt.

Glue, Codfish and Gent's Neckwear.

Undertaker and Confectioner.

}}"Diseases of Horses and Children a Specialty."

John White, Ptr.

The flames spread rapidly, until they threat ened the Palace rink of our esteemed fellow-townsman, Mr. Pendergast, whose genial and urbane manner has endeared him to all.

With a degree of forethought worthy of a better cause, Mr. Leroy W. Butts suggested the propriety of calling out the hook and ladder company, an organization of which every one seemed to be justly proud. Some delay ensued in trying to find the janitor of Pioneer Hook and Ladder Company No. 1's building, but at last he was secured, and after he had gone home for the key, Mr. Butts ran swiftly down the street to awake the foreman, but after he had dressed himself and inquired anxiously about the fire, he said that he was not foreman of the company since the 2d of April.

Meantime the fire-fiend continued to rise up ever and anon on his hind feet and lick up salt barrel after salt barrel in close proximity to the Palace rink, owned by our esteemed fellow-citizen, Mr. Pendergast. Twice Mr. Pendergast was seen to shudder, after which he went home and filled out a blank which he forwarded to the insurance company.

Just as the town seemed doomed the hook-and-ladder company came rushing down the street with their navy-blue hook-and-ladder truck. It is indeed a beauty, being one of the Excelsior noiseless hook-and-ladder factory's best instruments, with tall red pails and rich blue ladders.

Some delay ensued, as several of the officers claimed that under a new by-law passed in January they were permitted to ride on the truck to fires. This having been objected to by a gentleman who had lived in Chicago for several years, a copy of the by-laws was sent for and the dispute summarily settled. The company now donned its rubber overcoats with great coolness and proceeded at once to deftly twist the tail of the fire-fiend.

It was a thrilling sight as James McDonald, a brother of Terrance McDonald, Trombone, Ind., rapidly ascended one of the ladders in the full glare of the devouring element and fell off again.

Then a wild cheer rose to a height of about nine feet, and all again became confused.

It was now past 11 o'clock, and several of the members of the hook-and-ladder company who had to get up early the next day in order to catch a train excused themselves and went home to seek much-needed rest.

Suddenly it was discovered that the brick livery stables of Mr. McMichaels, a nephew of our worthy assessor, was getting hot. Leaving the Palace rink to its fate, the hook-and-ladder company directed its attention to the brick barn, and after numerous attempts at last succeeded in getting its large iron prong fastened on the second story window-sill, which was pulled out. The hook was again inserted but not so effectively, bringing down this time an armful of hay and part of an old horse blanket. Another courageous jab was made with the iron hook, which succeeded in pulling out about five cents' worth of brick. This was greeted by a wild burst of applause from the bystanders, during which the hook-and-ladder company fell over each other and added to the horror of the scene by a mad burst of pale-blue profanity.

It was not long before the stable was licked up by the fire-fiend, and the hook-and-ladder company directed its attention toward the undertaking, embalming, and ice-cream parlors of our highly-esteemed fellow-townsman, Mr. A. Burlingame. The company succeeded in pulling two stone window-sills out of this building before it burned. Both times they were encored by the large and aristocratic audience.

Mr. Burlingame at once recognized the efforts of the heroic firemen by tapping a keg of beer, which he distributed among them at twenty-five cents per glass.

This morning a space forty-seven feet wide, where but yesterday all was joy and prosperity and beauty, is covered over with blackened ruins. Mr. Pendergast is overcome by grief at the loss of his rink, but assures us that if he is successful in getting the full amount of his insurance he will take the money and build two rinks, either one of which will be far more imposing than the one destroyed last evening.

A movement is on foot to give a literary and musical entertainment at Burley's Hall to raise funds for the purchase of new uniforms for the "fire laddies," at which Mrs. Butts has consented to sing "When the Robins Nest Again," and Miss Mertie Stout will recite "'Ostler Joe," a selection which never fails to offend the best people everywhere. Twenty-five cents for each offence. Let there be a full house.

BIG STEVE

YOU think, no doubt, William, that I am happy, but I cannot say that I am. I will tell you my little reminiscence if you don't mind, and you can judge for yourself." These were the words of Big Steve, as we sat together one evening, watching the dealer slide the cards out of his little tin photograph album, while the crowd bought chips of the banker and corded them up out the green table.

"You look on me as a great man to inaugurate a funeral, and wish that you had a miscellaneous cemetery yourself to look back on; but greatness always has its drawbacks. We cannot be great unless we pay the price. What we call genius is after all only industry and perseverance. When my father undertook to clean me out, in our own St. Lawrence County home, I filed his coat-tails full of bird-shot and fled. Father afterwards said that he could have overlooked it so far as the coat was concerned, but he didn't want it shot to pieces while he had it on.

"Then I went to Kansas City and shot a colored man. That was a good many years ago, and you could kill a colored man then as you can a Chinaman now, with impunity, or any other weapon you can get your hands onto. Still the colored man had friends and I had to go further West. I went to Nevada then, and lived under a cloud and a *nom de plume,* as you fellers say.

"I really didn't want to thin out the population of Nevada, but I had to protect myself. They say that after a feller has killed his man, he has a thirst for blood and can't stop, but that ain't so. You 'justifiable-homicide' a man and get clear, and then you have to look out for friends of the late lamented. You see them everywhere. If your stomach gets out of order you see the air full of vengeance, and you drink too much and that don't help it. Then you kill a man on suspicion that he is follering you up, and after that you shoot in an extemporaneous, way, that makes life in your neighborhood a little uncertain.

"That's the way it was with me. I've got where I don't sleep good any more, and the fun of life has kind of pinched out, as we say in the mines. It's a big thing to run a school-meeting or an election, but it hardly pays me for the free spectacular show I see when I'm trying to sleep. You know if you've ever killed a man—"

"No, I never killed one right out," I said apologetically. "I shot one once, but he gained seventy-five pounds in less than six months."

"Well, if you ever had, you'd notice that he always says or does something that you can remember him by. He either says, 'Oh, I am shot'! or 'You've killed me'! or something like that, in a reproachful way, that you can wake up in the night and hear most any time. If you kill him dead, and he don't say a word, he will fall hard on the ground, with a groan that will never stop. I can shut my eyes and hear one now. After you've done it, you always wish they'd showed a little more fight. You could forgive 'em if they'd cuss you, and holler, and have some style about 'em, but they won't. They just reel, and fall, and groan. Do you know I can't eat a meal unless my back is agin' the wall. I asked Wild Bill once how he could stand it to turn his back on the crowd and eat a big dinner. He said he generally got drunk just before dinner, and that helped him out.

"So you see, William, that if a man is a great scholar, he is generally dyspeptic; if he's a big preacher, they tie a scandal to his coat-tail, and if he's an eminent murderer, he has insomnia and loss of appetite. I almost wish sometimes that I had remained in obscurity. Its a big thing to be a public man, with your name in the papers and everybody afraid to collect a bill of you, for fear you'll let the glad sunlight into their thorax; but when you can't eat nor sleep, and you're liable to wake up with your bosom full of buckshot, or your neck pulled out like a turkey-gobler's, and your tongue hanging out of your mouth in a ludicrous manner, and your overshoes failing to touch the ground by about ten feet, you begin to look back on your childhood and wish you could again be put there, sleepy and sinless, hungry and happy."

SPEECH OF RED SHIRT, THE FIGHTING CHIEF OF THE SIOUX NATION

IT HAD been a day of triumph at Erastina. Buffalo Bill, returning from Marlborough House, had amused the populace with the sports of an amphitheatre to an extent hitherto unknown even in that luxurious city. A mighty multitude of people from Perth Amboy and New York had been present to watch the attack on the Dead wood coach and view with bated breath the conflict in the arena.

The shouts of revelry had died away. The last loiterer had retired from the bleaching boards and the lights in the palace of the cowboy band were extinguished. The moon piercing the tissue of fleecy clouds, tipped the dark waters about Constable Hook with a wavy, tremulous light. The dark-browed Roman soldier, wearing an umbrella belonging to Imre Kiralfy, wabbled slowly homeward, the proud possessor of a large rectangular "jag."

No sound was heard save the low sob of some retiring wave as it told its story to the smooth pebbles of the beach, or the lower sob of some gentleman who had just sought to bed down a brand-new bucking bronco from Ogallalla and decided to escape violently through the roof of the tent; then all was still as the breast when the spirit has departed. Anon the smoke-tanned Cheyenne snore would steal in upon the silence and then die away like the sough of a summer breeze. In the green-room of the amphitheatre a little band of warriors had assembled. The foam of conflict yet lingered on their lips, the scowl of battle yet hung upon their brows, and the large knobs on their classic profiles indicated that it had been a busy day with them. The night wynd blew chill and the warrior had added to his moss-agate ear-bobs a heavy coat of maroon-colored roof paint.

There was an embarrassing silence of a little spell and then Red Shirt, fighting chief of the Sioux Nation borrowed a chew of tobacco from Aurelius Poor Doe, stepped forth and thus addressed them:

Fellow-Citizens and Gentlemen of the Wild West: Ye call me chief, and ye do well to call him chief who for two long years has met in the arena every shape of man or beast that the broad empire of Nebraska could furnish, and yet has never lowered his arm.

If there be one among you can say that ever at grub dance or scalp german or on the war-path my action did belie my tongue let him stand forth and say it and I will send him home with his daylights done up in the morning paper. If there be three in all your company dare face me on the bloody sands let them come on and I will bore holes in the arena with them and utilize them in fixing up a sickening spectacle.

And yet I was not alway thus, a hired butcher attacking a Deadwood coach, both afternoon and evening, the savage chief of still more savage men.

My ancestors came from Illinois. They dwelt there in the vine-clad hills and citron groves of the Sangamon at a time when the country was overrun with Indians. Instead of paying to see Indians, my ancestors would walk a long distance over a poor road in order to get a shot at a white man.

In Dakota my early life ran quiet as the clear brook by which I babbled, and my boyhood was one long, happy summer day. We bathed in the soiled waters of the upper Missouri and ate the luscious prickly pear in the land of the Dakotahs.

I did not then know what war was, but when Sitting Bull told me of Marathon and Leuctra and Bull Run, and how at a fortified railroad pass Imre Kiralfy had withstood the whole Roman army, my cheek burned, I knew not why, and I thought what a glorious thing it would be to leave the reservation and go upon the warpath. But my mother kissed my throbbing temples and bade me go soak my head and think no more of those old tales and savage wars.

That very night the entire regular army and wife landed on our coasts. They tore down our tepee, stampeded our stock, stole our grease paints and played a mean trick on our dog.

To-day in the arena I killed a man in the Black Hills coach, and when I undid his cinch, behold! he was my friend. The same sweet smile was on his face that I had noted when I met him on my trip abroad. He knew me smiled faintly, made a few false motions and died. I begged that I might bear away the body to my tepee and express it to his country seat, near Limerick, and upon my bended knees, amid the dust and blood of the arena, I begged this pool favor, and a Roman prætor from St. George answered: "Let the carrion rot. There are no noble men but Romans and banana men. Let the show go on. Give us our money's worth. Bring out the bobtail lion from Abyssinia and the bucking bronco from Dead Man's Ranch." And the assembled maids and matrons and the rabble shouted in derision and told me to brace up, and bade Johnnie git his gun, git his gun, git his gun, and other vile flings which

I do not now recall. And so must you, fellow warriors, and so must I, die like dogs. Ye stand here like giants (N. Y. Giants) as ye are, but to-morrow the fangs of the infuriated buffalo may sink into your quivering flesh. To-night ye stand here in the full flush of health and conscious rectitude, but to-morrow some crank may shoot you from the Deadwood coach.

Hark! Hear ye yon buffalo roaring in her den? 'Tis three days since she tasted flesh, but to-morrow she will have warrior on toast, and don't you forget it. And she will fling your vertebrae about her cage like the costly Etruscan pitcher of a League nine.

If ye are brutes, then stand here like fat oxen waiting for the butcher's knife. If ye are men, arise and follow me. We will beat down the guard, overpower the ticket-chopper and cut for the tall timber. We will go through Ellum Park, Port Richmond, Tower Hill, West Brighton, Sailors' Snug Harbor and New Brighton like a colored revival through a watermelon patch, beat down the walls of the Circus Maximus, tear the mosquito bars from the windows of Nero's palace, capture the Roman ballet and light out for Europe.

O comrades! warriors!! gladiators!!!

If we be men, let us die like men, beneath the blue sky, don't you know, and by the still waters, according to Gunter, in the presence of the nobility, rather than be stepped on by a spoiled bronco, surrounded by low tradesmen from New York.

TO THE POOR SHINNECOCK

THERE can be nothing more pathetic than to watch the decay of a race, even though it be a scrub race. To watch the decay of the Indian race, has been with me, for many years a passion, and the more the Indian has decayed the more reckless I have been in studying his ways.

The Indian race for over two hundred years has been a race against Time, and I need hardly add that Time is away ahead as I pen these lines.

I dislike to speak of myself so much, but I have been identified with the Indians more or less for fifteen years. In 1876 I was detailed by a San Francisco paper to attend the Custer massacre and write it up, but not knowing where the massacre was to be held I missed my way and wandered for days in an opposite direction. When I afterwards heard how successful the massacre was, and fully realized what I had missed, my mortification knew no bounds, but I might have been even more so if I had been successful. We never know what is best for us.

But the Indian is on the wane, whatever that is. He is disappearing from the face of the earth, and we find no better illustration of this sad fact than the gradual fading away of the Shinnecock Indians near the extremity of Long Island.

In company with *The World* artist, who is paid a large salary to hold me up to ridicule in these columns, I went out the other day to Southampton and visited the surviving members of this great tribe.

Neither of us knows the meaning of fear. If we had been ordered by the United States Government to wipe out the whole Shinnecock tribe we would have taken a damp towel and done it.

The Shinnecock tribe now consists of James Bunn and another man. But they are neither of them pure-blooded Shinnecock Indians. One-Legged Dave, an old whaler, who, as the gifted reader has no doubt already guessed, has but one leg, having lost the other in going over a reef many years ago, is a pure-blooded Indian, but not a pure-blooded Shinnecock. Most of these Indians are now mixed up with the negro race by marriage and are not considered warlike.

The Shinnecocks have not been rash enough to break out since they had the measles some years ago, but we will let that pass.

There are now about 150 Shinnecocks on the reservation, the most of whom are negroes. They live together in peace and hominy, trying most of the time to ascertain what the wild waves are saying in regard to fish.

There is an air of gentle, all-pervading peace which hangs over the Shinnecock hills and that had its effect even upon my tumultuous and aggressive nature, wooing me to repose. I could rest there all this summer and then, after a good night's sleep, I could go right at it again in the morning. Rest at Southampton does not seem to fatigue one as it does elsewhere.

The Shinnecock Indian has united his own repose of manner with the calm and haughty distrust of industry peculiar to the negro, and the result is something that approaches nearer to the idea of eternal rest than anything I have ever seen. The air seems to be saturated with it and the moonlight is soaked full of calm. It would be a good place in which to wander through the gloaming and pour a gallon or so of low, passionate yearning into the ear of a loved one.

As a friend of mine, who is the teacher of modern languages and calisthenics in an educational institution, once said, "the air seems filled with that delicious dolce farina for which those regions is noted for." I use his language because I do not know now how I could add to it in any way.

We visited Mr. James Bunn at his home on Huckleberry avenue, saw the City Hall and Custom House and obtained a front view of it, secured a picture of the residence of the Street Commissioner and then I talked with Mr. Bunn while the artist got a marine view of his face.

Mr. Bunn was for forty years a whaler, but had abandoned the habit now, as there is so little demand among the restaurants for whales, and also because there are fewer whales. I ascertained from him that the whale at this season of the year does not readily rise to the fly, but bites the harpoon greedily during the middle of the day.

Mr. Bunn also gave us a great deal of other Information, among other things informing us of the fact that the white men had been up to their old tricks and were trying to steal portions of the reservation that had not been nailed down. He did not say whether it was the same man who is trying to steal the old Southampton graveyard or not.

James is about seventy-five years old and his father once lived in a wigwam on the Shinnecock Hills. Mr. Bunn says that the country has changed very much in the past 250 years and that I would hardly know the place if I could have seen it at first. During that time he says two other houses have been built and he has reshingled the L of his barn with hay.

He told us the thrilling story of the Spanish Sylph and how she was wrecked many years ago on the coast near his house, and how the Spanish dollars burst out of her gaping side and fell with a low, mellow plunk into the raging main.

How and then the sea has given up one of these "sand-dollars" as the years went by, and not over two years ago one was found along the shore near by. What I blame the Shinnecock Indians for is their fatal yearning to subsist solely on this precarious income.

But with the decline of the whaling industry, due somewhat to the great popularity of natural and acquired gas as a lubricant, together with the cheap methods of picking up electricity and preserving it for illuminating purposes, and also to the fact that whales are more skittish than they used to be, the Shinnecock whaler is left high and dry.

It is, indeed, a pathetic picture. Here on the stern and rock-bound coast, where their ancestors greeted Columbus and other excursionists as they landed on the new dock and at once had their pictures taken in a group for the illustration on the greenbacks, now the surviving relic of a brave people, with bowed heads and frosting locks, are waiting a few days only for the long, dark night of merciful oblivion.

So he walks in the night-time, all through the long fly time, he walks by the sorrowful sea, and he yearns to wake never, but lie there forever in the arms of the sheltering sea, to lie in the lap of the sea.

At least that is my idea of the way the Shinnecock feels about it.

The Indian race, wherever we find it, gives us a wonderful illustration of the great, inherent power of rum as a human leveler. The Indian has, perhaps, greater powers of endurance than the white man, and enters into the great unequal fight with rum almost hilariously, but he loses his presence of mind and forgets to call a cab at the proper moment. This is a matter that has never been fully understood even by the pale face, and of course the Indian is a perfect child in the great conflict with rum. The result is that the Indian is passing away under our very eyes, and the time will soon come when the Indian agent will have to seek some other healthful, outdoor exercise.

So the consumptive Shinnecock, the author of "Shinny on Your Own Ground and Other Games," is soon to live only in the flea-bitten records of a great nation. Once he wrote pieces for the boys to speak in school, and contributed largely to McGuffy's and Sander's periodicals, but now you never hear of an Indian who is a good extemporaneous public speaker, or who can write for sour apples.

He no longer makes the statement that he is an aged hemlock, that his limbs are withered and his trunk attached by the constable. He has ceased to tell through the columns of the Fifth Reader how swift he used to be as a warrior and that the war-path is now overgrown with grass. He very seldom writes anything for the papers except over the signature of Veritas, and the able young stenographer who used to report his speeches at the council fire seems to have moved away.

Two hundred and fifty years ago the Shinnecock Hills were covered by a dense forest, but in that brief period, as if by magic, two and one-half acres of that ground have been cleared, which is an average of an entire acre for every hundred years. When we stop to consider that very little of this work was done by the women and that the men have to attend to the cleaning of the whales in order to prepare them for the table, and also write their contributions for the school-books and sign treaties with the White Father at Washington, we are forced to admit that had the Indian's life been spared for a few thousand years more he would have been alive at the end of that time.

So they wander on together, waiting for the final summons. Waiting for the pip or measles, and their cough is dry aud hacking as they cough along together towards the large and wide hereafter.

They have lived so near Manhattan, where refinement is so plenty, where the joy they jerk from barley — every other day but Sunday — gives the town a reddish color, that the Shinnecock is dying, dying with his cowhide boots on, dying with his hectic flush on, while the church bells chime in Brooklyn and New Yorkers go to Jersey, go to get their fire-water, go to get their red-eyed bug-juice, go to get their cooking whiskey.

Far away at Minnehaha, in the land of the Dakota, where the cyclone feels so kinky, rising on its active hind-feet, with its tail up o'er the dashboard, blowing babies through the grindstone without injuring the babies, where the cyclone and the whopper journey on in joy together — there refinement and frumenti, with the new and automatic maladies and choice diseases that belong to the Caucasian, gather in the festive red man, take him to the reservation, rob him while his little life lasts, rob him till he turns his toes up, rob him till he kicks the bucket.

And the Shinnecock is fading, he who greeted Chris. Columbus when he landed, tired and seasick, with a breath of peace and onions; he who welcomed other strangers, with their notions of refinement and their knowledge of the Scriptures and their fondness for Gambrinus—they have compassed his damnation and the Shinnecock is busted.

WEBSTER AND HIS GREAT BOOK

NOAH Webster probably had the best command of language of any author of our time. Those who have read his great work entitled Webster's Unabridged Dictionary, or How One Word Led to Another, will agree with me that he was smart. Noah never lacked for a word by which to express himself. He was a brainy man and a good speller.

We were speaking of Mr. Webster on the way up here this afternoon, and a gentleman from Ashland told me of his death. Those of you who have read Mr. Webster's works will be pained to learn of this. One by one our eminent men are passing away. Mr. Webster has passed away; Napoleon Bonaparte is no more, and Dr. Mary Walker is fading away. This has been a severe winter on Sitting Bull, and I have to guard against the night air a good deal myself.

It would ill become me at this late date to criticise Mr. Webster's work, a work that is now I may say in nearly every office, home, school-room and counting-room in the land. It is a great book. I only hope that had Mr. Webster lived he would have been equally fair in his criticism of my books.

I hate to compare my books with Mr. Webster's, because it looks egotistical in me; but although Noah's book is larger than mine and has more literary attractions as a book to set a child on at the table, it does not hold the interest of the reader all the way through.

He has tried to introduce too many characters into his book at the expense of the plot. It is a good book to pick up and while away a leisure hour, perhaps, but it is not a work that could rivet your interest till midnight, while the fire went out and the thermometer went down to 47 below zero. You do not hurry through the pages to see whether Reginald married the girl or not. Mr. Webster didn't seem to care whether he married the girl or not.

Therein consists the great difference between Noah and myself. He don't keep up the interest. A friend of mine at Sing Sing who secured one of my books, said he never left his room till he had devoured it. He said he seemed chained to the spot, and if you can't believe a convict who is entirely ont of politics, who in the name of George Washington can you believe?

Mr. Webster was certainly a most brilliant writer, but a little inclined, perhaps, to be wrong. I have discovered in some of his later books 118,000 words no two of which are alike. This shows great fluency and versatility, it is true, but we need something else. The reader waits in vain to be thrilled by the author's wonderful word-painting. There is not a thrill in the whole tome. Noah wasn't much of a thriller. I am free to confess that when I read this book, of which I had heard so much, I was bitterly disappointed. It is a larger book than mine and costs more, and has more pictures in it than mine, but is it a work that will make a man lead a different life? What does he say of the tariff? What does he say of the roller skating rink? He is silent. He is full of cold, hard words and dry definitions, but what does he say of the Mormons and female suffrage, and how to cure the pip? Nothing. He evades everything, just as a man does when he writes a letter accepting the nomination for President.

As I said before, however, it is a good book to pickup for a few moments or to read on the train. I could never think of taking a long r. r. journey without Mr. Webster's tale in my pocket. I would just as quick think of traveling without my bottle of cough medicine as to start out without Mr. Webster's book.

Mr. Webster's Speller was a work of less pretensions, perhaps, but it had an immense sale. Eight years ago 40,000,000 of these books had been sold, and yet it had the same grave defect. It was disconnected, cold, prosy and dull. I read it for years, and at last became a very close student of Mr. Webster's style. Still I never found but one thing in the book for which there was such a stampede, which was even ordinarily interesting, and that was a perfect gem. It was so thrilling in detail and so different from Mr. Webster's general style that I have often wondered who he got to write it for him. Perhaps it was the author of the *Bread Winners*. It related to the discovery of a boy in the crotch of an old apple tree by an elderly gentleman, and the feeling of bitterness and animosity that sprang up between the two, and how the old man told the boy at first that he had better come down out of that tree, because he was afraid the limb would break with him and let him fall. Then, as the boy still remained, he told him that those were not eating-apples, that they were just common cooking-apples, and that there were worms in them. But the boy said he didn't mind a little thing like that. So then the old gentleman got irritated and called the dog and threw turf at the boy, and at last saluted him with pieces of turf and decayed cabbages; and after he had gone away the old man pried the bulldog's jaws open and found a mouthful of pantaloons and a freckle. I do not tell this, of course, in Mr. Webster's language but I give the main points as they recur now to my mind.

Though I have been a close student of Mr. Webster for years and examined his style closely, I am free to say that his ideas about writing a book are not the same as mine. Of course it is a great temptation for a young author to write a book that will have a large sale, but that should not be all. We should have a higher object than that, and strive to interest those who read our books. It should not be jerky and scattering in its statements.

I do not wish to do an injustice to a great man who I learn is now no more, a man who has done so much for the world and who could spell the longest word without hesitation, but I speak of these things just as I would expect others to criticise nay work. If one aspire to monkey with the *literati* of our day we must expect to be criticised. I have been criticised myself. When I was in public life—as a justice of the peace in the Rocky Mountains—a man came in one day and criticised me so that I did not get over it for two weeks.

I might add, though I dislike to speak of it now, that Mr. Webster was at one time a member of the Legislature of Massachusetts. I believe that was the only time he ever stepped aside from the straight and narrow way. A good many people do not know this, but it is true. It only shows how a good man may at one time in his life go wrong.